Quilting

A MODERN CREATIVE JOURNEY
THROUGH AN AGE-OLD CRAFT

Andrea Tsang Jackson

9/10

PUBLICATIONS

VANCOUVER

Nine Ten Publications Inc.
Vancouver
ninetenpublications.ca

Library and Archives Canada Cataloguing in Publication

Title: Quilting : a modern creative journey through an age-old craft /
    Andrea Tsang Jackson.
Names: Tsang Jackson, Andrea, author
Description: Includes bibliographical references and index.
Identifiers:
    Canadiana (print) 20240516400 |
    Canadiana (ebook) 20240516761 | ISBN 9781777387099
    (softcover) | ISBN 9781738360703 (PDF)
Subjects: LCSH: Quilting—Technique. | LCSH: Quilting—Patterns.
Classification: LCC TT835 .T736 2025 | DDC 746.46—dc23

Editing by Kim Werker
Technical Editing by Jessica Schunke
Copyediting by Michelle Woodvine
Proofreading by Lianne Johnsen
Indexing by Marnie Lamb
Book and Cover Design by Ninth and May Design Co.
Cover Photo by Shaeline Faith Photography

Production of this book was made possible by the enthusiasm and financial support of readers and quilt lovers who backed the project on Kickstarter. Without you, dearest backers, this book would not exist. Thank you!

Visit shop.ninetenpublications.ca for more books and booklets about how to make things, how things are made, and where our art and craft materials come from.

Printed and bound in Canada on 100% post-consumer waste recycled Sustana Enviro Satin paper, which is processed chlorine-free. It is designated Ancient Forest Friendly™ and FSC® certified.

  PCF

To today's quilters and the quilters before and after us—
you are our community.

—A. T. J.

Contents

Foreword

Immediately after reading an early draft of this book I went to my stash and started cutting fabric. I had an idea, an itch that needed scratching. It happens that way sometimes. The idea comes into your head and you just can't let it go. You might jot down some notes, even draw a quick sketch, but it isn't as satisfying as getting your hands wrapped up in some fabric.

Quilting is lovely book designed to get you thinking and playing within your personal quilting practice. The word "playing" is mine. I may live in a quilt world heavily improvised, but Andrea suggests a more structured, but not terribly different approach. "Testing in a low-stakes environment," as she says. Andrea shows us how to explore our confidence in quilting and embrace our journeys with the art and craft of it.

The first time I met Andrea was in a fabric store many years ago. She invited me to meet her at Patch Halifax while I was in town on a teaching gig with the Maritime Modern Quilt Guild. She may disagree, but I sensed nervousness as she told me about writing her first book and asked me questions about the quilting industry. Now she is a strong, confident quilt artist. She's taken her career to really interesting places and I love getting surprised by each move.

Andrea's never been one to stop moving forward. Life brings its pauses or interruptions, yet she is always exploring her creativity. She started with quilts, designed patterns, and could have been very successful in the world of fabric in lap form. But she pushed both herself and the boundaries of what is a quilt. We've seen her experiment with wedding dresses, large-scale art, installations in materials other than fabric, and yes, new-to-her techniques in quilting. Each time it comes from a development of her curiosity. A "what if" moment. Or an "I wonder" moment.

For a lot of us, doing just one of these things, or even one step of one of these things, is terrifying. Not like standing on a glass floor 100 stories up kind of terrifying, but because we often lack the confidence to try the new thing. Or, for some strange reason as quilters who will likely never run out of fabric, because we are afraid of wasting fabric. It might be, if we dig down a little, because we are afraid of failing or of squandering our time; that an orphan block that never made it to be a quilt is somehow symbolic of us being a bad person. Does every artist's sketch make it onto a gallery wall? Does every kid's drawing get put on the fridge? Of course not, so why do we think everything we sew has to make it into a quilt? Quilting is a low-stakes game, as Andrea reminds us, so any kind of experimentation with our fabric is a done in a low-stakes environment. We will all do well to keep this perspective in mind.

The Quests in this book, as Andrea lays them out, are a perfect way to explore quilting and build confidence. You don't have to make the quilt, any quilt. You can just try on a few ideas and see if they work for you. And if they don't? Well then, you tried them. It isn't a failure, it was an investment in your creative confidence.

The idea I played with, the creative itch I had to scratch, came as a result of exploring two of the Quests. I had the advantage of reading the book without any pictures. While a bit of a challenge when it comes to a quilt book, it did allow my mind to wander. So with *House* and *Fogo II* my imagination went to some fun places. I revisited a project or two I'd started during the pandemic—when home meant something special and safe—and I dreamed of winter and ice.

With the fabric I pulled, I cut, sewed, pressed, and sewed some more. An idea became a few blocks. I interpreted (or misinterpreted) Andrea's descriptions into something that became my own, yet inspired by her words. I had no obligation to produce a thing, only to experiment a little. What I made did not match what I had in my head when I started. In fact, it felt like I veered from my intentions quite a bit. Notice I didn't call it a mistake. It just came out differently. After the first few blocks I could have been mad that it wasn't working. I could have chucked the blocks in the scrap bin. I could have chastised myself for wasting time. Instead, I put them up on the design wall and asked myself what I liked about them, and, yes, what didn't work. In the end, I liked more than I disliked. Plus, I didn't really care that my original idea wasn't realized. Then I tried again, learning and leaning into what I did in the first place.

The whole time I had Andrea's voice in the back of my head.

"When we let go of control of the processes and the outcomes, we will experience something new that we couldn't have orchestrated for ourselves."

It doesn't matter if the blocks I made become a quilt. I ran out of fabric, if I am being totally honest. The exploration, however, was eye-opening. For one, being inspired by another person is a fascinating experience. You want to pay homage to them yet still do your own thing. Secondly, when things don't turn out as you pictured them in your head it can be demoralizing, so you have to make a conscious decision to see the time spent as a worthwhile experiment. And finally, even when you are at the part of the process where you think it should all be chucked in the scrap bin, you've got to remember that it was all still an investment in your creative confidence.

Building confidence happens—pardon the cliché—one stitch at a time. With each block, each quilt, your skills get better. Not only that, you get better. You learn more about yourself, your desires, your frustrations, your joys. *Quilting* is a guide for examining and understanding the *why* of that growth and change. If you've never taken the time to experiment or examine your whys when it comes to quilting, now is the time to explore. Use this book as your guide.

CHERYL ARKISON
July, 2024
Calgary

Quilting: A Modern Creative Journey Through an Age-Old Craft

Introduction

ORIGINS

I grew up in a quilt-less home. Coziness and sentimentality were not highly valued in the family that I come from. But before you feel sorry for me, know that I grew up in a home that was full of safety and security. Those were values held in high regard and were equated with love; my sense of freedom to try new things comes from these values. The new things were not in the realm of climbing mountains[1] or deep-sea diving, but rather trying new foods, learning a new skill (usually a craft skill because that's where my interests led), or taking on a leadership role at school. My confidence grew with every new experience, like a muscle getting stronger the more I used it.

Leaving the safety of my home, I set off to architecture school and a different world opened up for me. Architecture was a great education. It sat in the middle of a Venn diagram of disciplines: science, engineering, art, craft, economics, politics, and history. It was a wonderful way to learn about the world and how it worked. Moreover, it was empowering. To me, design is agency; it is a way to imagine a reality that doesn't exist yet and then take steps to move toward it, no matter how epic or inconsequential the final building or

Opposite:
Crow Quills Analog
2014
45" × 60"
(114 cm × 152 cm)
Photo credit:
Deborah Wong

---

1   I eventually walked up a mountain, with the help of mildly sloped switchbacks and a cheerleading husband.

product is. Design is solving a problem. From then on, I saw everything as a design problem to be solved. What to eat for dinner, how to plan a wedding, how to set up a system so kids' gloves don't get lost, how to make a quilt, how to teach a workshop, how to write an art proposal. Design became a framework for moving through life.

My quilting journey began in 2011, when I was expecting my first child. It was what I assumed a quilt should look like: blocks in a grid with sashing, cornerstones, and borders albeit with a contemporary colour palette of grey, white, orange, and yellow. But it was my second quilt that became the beginning of something more. I started my *Crow Quills Analog* (page 10) quilt when I was pregnant with my second child, and over the course of twenty-two months, I collected twenty-five different solid fabrics and assembled them into a quilt of more than 2,000 triangles that became more than 500 hourglass blocks. At the time, I had no idea what an hourglass block was and I individually cut out each triangle and sewed four into a square. They were meticulously placed into a seemingly random arrangement based on an untitled work by illustrator Andy Gilmore created in 2010. Although I didn't consider myself a quilter until a few years later, that second quilt spoke to me. The solid fabrics, the endless shades of colour and delightful adjacencies, the repetitive nature of the cutting and assembly, the flow state that I entered when I was working—where time stood still and also went on forever—it was all very appealing.

When I made *Crow Quills Analog* I didn't know there was such a thing as modern quilting, but as soon as I discovered it (probably through a blog because I wasn't on Instagram then), I knew this was where my aesthetic preferences sat very comfortably. I was attracted to solid fabrics—without the "ornament" that I had been taught to consider superfluous and unnecessary. A certain minimalism, where every shape and stitch is essential, was, and still is, what I am naturally drawn to. Limited colour palettes, ample negative space, asymmetry...these are all part of my mother (or, in the case of male-dominated modernist and minimalist design and art, *father*) tongue.

As I first began to explore modern quilting, I was very interested in geometry. I tried to make fabric act like an idealized material with strict geometry, sharp edges, and facets. My first book, *Patchwork Lab: Gemology*, was a book of gemstone patterns constructed with foundation paper piecing. My approach was

Family Circle from *Patchwork Lab: Gemology* (Lucky Spool, 2019). 68" × 68" (173 cm × 173 cm). Quilted by Sheri Lund, Violet Quilts.

In Conversation, 2022. Parkade artwork in Halifax, Nova Scotia. Photo credit: Deborah Wong.

like that of most craft and quilting books—didactic, with specific outcomes. It was a lab, not for experimentation, but for teaching the reader what I knew in the most direct, clear, and predictable way. That book came out several years and a pandemic ago. I have taken a decidedly different approach with the book you're reading now: Rather than explicitly teaching you to make a particular quilt, my goal is to provide insights and exercises that invite you to discover what draws you to quilting. Here, you'll find many more organic shapes and even some print fabric. The Quests—the project-oriented portion of the book—are a little messier, raw edges are left raw and loose ends are not always tied up. I try to lean into realities rather than the idealized. When I began creating this book, I encouraged myself, as I now encourage you, to surrender to the material, the process, and the idea, rather than be enslaved to a pre-determined outcome.

My previous experiences in architecture and design always had me thinking about how quilts exist in space. How they crumple on a couch or hang with wobbly edges against a wall. Quilts sit—rightly—in the domestic sphere; they are closely associated with home and comfort. But I had a desire to see quilts outside these conventions. Quilts don't tend to exist in public spaces because the fragility of textiles makes it difficult for them to stand up well to the elements or even the natural light that filters into an indoor space. I thought there surely must be a way. For most of my quilting career, I have had this question loom over me, and in the last few years, I have found opportunities to explore how textiles can exist in public spaces, either as the textiles themselves or as representations and translations of them. *In Conversation*, pictured above, is an example of the work that I have begun to do in this vein.

I Am Not an Artist

On my kindergarten report card, my teacher observed that I really enjoyed making crafts. I can't remember a single craft that I made in kindergarten, but the observation tracked throughout the rest of my childhood and adolescence—decades before I ever started sewing seriously. In my teenage years, I especially liked paper craft and making beaded jewellery and would spend hours in my room, making things. I saw myself as creative, but not artistic. I thought of *artistic* as a term reserved for the more traditionally artistic media: drawing and painting.

In my mind's eye, an artistic child spends every spare moment with a pencil and sketchbook in hand, making detailed drawings and rendering them with such finesse that they jump off the page. I was not that child. I could spend hours in my room *making*—stringing tiny beads into jewellery, designing and constructing a pop-up book for a school project, picking out magazine photographs with large swaths of one colour and collaging those solid colours and gradients into geometric collages to decorate my agenda, creating handmade valentines for all my friends. But drawing wasn't a medium that held any allure for me; I didn't feel like I had any natural talent for it. Painting was too messy and too much cleanup for my cleaning-averse self. So I didn't consider myself artistic. Crafty and creative, yes, but artistic, no.

I gave my quilt business and design studio the name "3rd Story Workshop." *Workshop* is a broad, non-discipline-specific term. At the time of its inception, and even a few years into it, I spent a great deal of energy thinking about the definitions of craft and fine craft, the boundaries of art, and what differentiates art from craft from design. Along with these considerations came questions about where I fit and how my work would be perceived—by the public, by artists, by designers, by craftspeople. It was easy calling myself a designer, because I was trained as such. I had two pieces of fancy paper telling me that I had spent many sleepless nights in a studio gluing bits of cardboard together and frantically drafting buildings using CAD (computer-aided design) software. Design is the way I think about problems and "designer" is an identity that fits like a glove.

There were distinctive moments when other monikers came to fit, too. I felt I could call myself a quilter once I joined a guild; I felt I could call myself an artist when I did my first artist residency and got my first artist grant; I could call myself a quilt designer once I released my first pattern. And I went about collecting these labels like McDonald's Happy Meal toys: a crafter, a maker, a creative, a designer, a quilter, an artist, a business owner, a freelancer. Depending on who I'm speaking to, I still use these terms to describe myself and what I do, but I don't fuss about them as much anymore. I just ask questions that I'm interested in and then go about finding the answers through quilting and craft, in different contexts and at different scales.

Another thing I don't dwell on anymore is a unified aesthetic or a style. Some quilters have a very recognizable style—a consistent colour palette, a signature technique, a discernible facet of quilting they delve into (for example, foundation paper piecing, free

Duchesse lace carved into acrylic, 2024.

motion quilting, hand quilting). You'll see that the projects in this book vary greatly. I set out with a question or a series of questions and parameters that I aim to work within. In my own work over the last few years, a theme that has emerged is the act of translation—taking the language of one medium and moving it to another. Craft media rendered as fabric designs and blown up to the scale of buildings. Drawing details of handmade lace and using a CNC (computer numerical control) machine to carve it in acrylic. This idea of translation comes up in the essay, *Building Containers* (page 30), which leads to the design for *Trellis* (page 78) and then *Still Life* (page 92).

Many of the things I talk about in this book are relevant to anyone who pursues a craft or anyone who simply enjoys creating— a person who journals, an amateur poet, a creative cook. But this book is written specifically for quilters. It's for the quilter who hesitates to call themselves an artist, but inside wonders if they are. Although my aesthetic preferences lean toward the modern, this book is for any quilter who not only creates beautiful things, but also reflects on their very personal relationship to their craft.

Belonging

I have a certain posture toward tradition; it is both reverent and irreverent. Perhaps this is a more pleasant way to say that I take and leave what I please. I lean on what I find to be most valuable: traditional quilt blocks and traditions of quilting in community. Quilt blocks are based on simple geometry, a solid age-old and cross-disciplinary foundation on which to express myself. And quilting communities give us a shared experience from which to build relationships and connections. They are a place for me to be myself.

I take these ideas as values to guide me rather than as rules to follow. I like how rooted it makes me feel, like my work is anchored in something that's outside of myself and not just centred on my whims.

One of the themes that comes out in my work is the idea of belonging. Where do I fit? Where do people, generally, fit and belong? Where does my work fit? When I think about belonging to a quilting community, I think about my quilting friends, my local guild, my global modern quilting community, but also about my community that spans time—before me and after me. This comes out most in the modern traditional design of *Trellis*, which uses the structure of the traditional *Irish Chain* quilt pattern to organize an exploration of line. The collective nature of *House* allows for different expressions of a single form within a group of quilters.

Five Quests: *Trellis, Still Life, House, Era: Boler,* and *Fogo II.*

Another aspect of belonging is rooted in a physical place. Many creative people are inspired by nature in its beauty and splendour. For me, a place is also a culture. How the people are in a place is directly related to the natural surroundings and climate they experience everyday, the local communities they engage in, and the histories that they bring with them from other places. *Fogo II* and *Era* aim to capture a sense of place and time, respectively. *Fogo II* is the physical manifestations of my experiences of a culture and a place. My version of *Era* is inspired by a memory of a time decades in the past and a dream for the future of travelling and adventure.

WHY THIS BOOK

In 2018, I wrote a three-fold mission statement to help me be intentional about the things I spent my creative energy on. One of the prongs of this mission was "to help people along in their creative journeys." Every quilt pattern I have designed aims to challenge the quilter, even if in the tiniest of ways: to establish a scant quarter-inch seam allowance, to create a transparency effect, to try improv within a block, to learn how to make quarter-square triangles. This book falls into this category of helping people along in the biggest way I understand it: to help quilters design their own creative journeys.

As we embark on these journeys, I want you to feel that same sense of security I felt growing up. That you have a place to come back to if you try something and it doesn't quite work out. That your worth is not tied up in the journey's outcome, but in the fact that you embarked on the journey in the first place. Safety is the birthplace of agency. From that place of safety and familiarity, I hope that you find the freedom to build your own quilting language, a way to articulate what you want to express. And I hope that freedom fuels the confidence that you can express your creative self well.

No matter how far I wander with my questions about craft, public space, culture, and community, I always come back to quilting. A nine-patch block, an HST (half-square triangle), a sawtooth star—these are places of comfort, reset, and rejuvenation.

Because what we do as quilters is of utmost importance, and at the same time, not important at all. My friend Duane Jones, who is an artist and also a basketball player, agrees that art and sport are the same in this regard. Each embodies something important: the stuff that life is made of; the place where our passions lie. It's what we work for. It's what we obsess about. It's what we enjoy most and where some of our best memories lie. It's what we live for.

HOW TO USE THIS BOOK

The first section of this book is a collection of five essays. They originated as part of a lecture I gave at virtual QuiltCon Together in 2021 and at the time I called them the "Strands of Quilting." Then, they were mere seeds—a few sentences each about five aspects of quilting. All of them might be present in your quilting life; some may be more dominant than others. The essays are short and easy to read. You might want to read them all in one sitting, or read them one at a time, spaced out over days or weeks. Either way, I recommend a warm beverage and a cookie[2] or chocolate truffle to go along with the reading.

The second section of the book is an Atlas containing Quests. These are prompts and projects that combine and explore the essays' ideas in an applied way. They can involve small experiments to try or whole quilts to make, depending on which path you choose. Most do not have precise fabric requirements or explicit finished dimensions. They are designed for you to try on something new and see if it "fits." The best way to approach the Quests is with an open hand and an open mind. They are invitations to exercise the muscle of trying new things, without putting too much on the line.

As far as materials are concerned, if you have been a quilter for any amount of time, you will have almost everything you need already, except maybe some jersey, fusible bias tape, a twin needle, and some specific interfacing. Otherwise, use what you have. If you are newer to quilting, you will be able to use leftover scraps from previous projects to start, thrift some materials, or purchase small amounts to try something out. If you are part of a guild that has a "free" table, this is the perfect place to acquire some materials and tools to play around with. ⚒

2 My favourite recipe is Martha Stewart's *Soft and Chewy Chocolate Chip Cookies*. I've used it for more than twenty years. It's heavy on the vanilla, which makes me feel like a kid in the best possible way. https://www.marthastewart.com/344840/soft-and-chewy-chocolate-chip-cookies. Updated July 5, 2023.

Creativity Manifesto

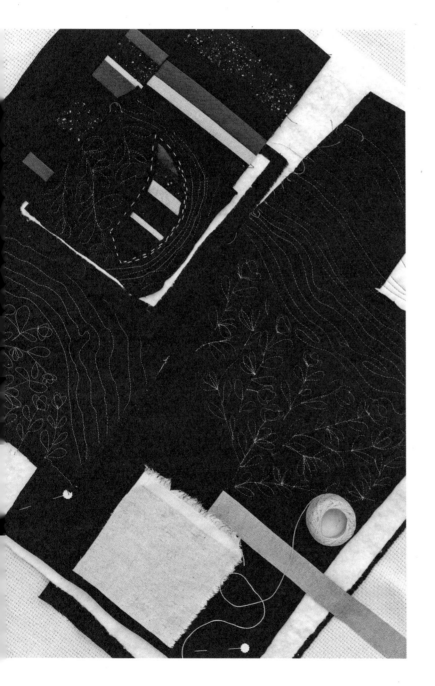

Creativity is versatile. It is so deeply human and I believe every human is creative. I can, without issue, describe a musician, an accountant, and a basketball player as creative in the same breath. For me, the source of our human creativity is a divine Creator that we reflect; for you, it may rest on another belief.

As I mentioned in the introduction, I resisted calling myself an artist for a while. I'm creative, without a doubt. You don't have to be a self-proclaimed artist to be creative. If you are more comfortable with the term "creative" or "quilter" rather than "artist," then go ahead and use the word you prefer. If you think of your work as craft or art—it doesn't matter too much, as long as you do it.

Artifacts of Andrea's design process as she worked on the quilt that would become the cover of this book.

Creativity is *making an omelette from scraps in the fridge.*
Creativity is *making up a game so that a child can understand a new idea.*
Creativity is *making a spreadsheet so your finances make sense.*
Creativity is *making an unexpected move to best an opponent.*

Creativity is *telling a story.*
Creativity is *crafting a quippy one-liner.*
Creativity is *withholding bits of a story only to later unleash all its power.*
Creativity is *seeing the long game while living the moment.*

Creativity is *observing beauty and simply taking it in, so that it turns up later as a powerful memory.*
Creativity is *working with randomness and intention.*
Creativity is *holding the tension between what is now and what could be.*
Creativity is *folding the past into the future and vice versa.*

Creativity is *exercising agency where none is given.*
Creativity is *understanding fiction as a testing plane.*
Creativity is *taking a risk and failing.*
Creativity is *mitigating risk.*
Creativity is *resiliency.*
Creativity is *trying again in hopes of even a marginally better outcome.*
Creativity is *turning the world upside down in the smallest and largest of ways.*
Creativity is *experimenting.*
Creativity is *experiencing fear.*
Creativity is *unquantifiable work.*

Creativity is *making something out of nothing.*
Creativity is *taking care of the mind, the body, and the spirit.*
Creativity *does not matter at all and it matters infinitely.*
Creativity is *without end.*

Order in Chaos

The world can be an utterly chaotic place. A baby comes into the world—a single dot in a complex web of people, environments, objects, knowledge, emotions, expectations, and dreams. They are unconnected for a short moment, then quickly entangled in the chaos. And they spend the rest of their lives organizing themselves in relation to these moving elements of the web.

We are constantly trying to make sense of the world in its ever-changing chaotic state. When we organize, it makes more sense. When we take that chaos and impose a structure on it, we can move through it.

As an adult, I feel like I'm constantly in organization mode. I'm managing stuff: tidying spaces; sorting fabric, sewing supplies, and equipment; managing kids' seasonal clothes and outgrown things. I'm the manager of a food system, purchasing and preparing food that gets consumed, over and over. I'm scheduling my own life and coordinating multiple schedules in our household. I'm continually learning new things and integrating them into my existing knowledge, or I'm discarding new or old information.

One of the things that a creative practice can provide us with is a sense of order in chaos. We have a domain, however small, where we have a lot of say in how we structure our time, resources, and energy. We design a space for ourselves to navigate the different kinds of chaos that inhabit our world.

CHAOS #1: The Weather (Limitless Possibilities)

I live near the Atlantic Ocean in Halifax, Nova Scotia, in the northeast of North America; a place where four seasons can occur within a single day. We are constantly at the mercy of what the weather will bring. A winter jacket in the morning, shorts and tank top in the afternoon, and a raincoat as dusk arrives. The tail end of a hurricane can shut down power, schools, and city life for a few days. We have to be prepared for anything. We live under the assumption that we don't have control over the weather, and moreover, that it dictates our actions and activities. These living conditions create a humble people and a sense of community, which I appreciate deeply and feel fortunate to be a part of.

But I often wonder what it is like to live in a climate that is consistent for 365 days of the year. Sunshine, flip-flops, being outside, just walking out the door without putting on a jacket or special footwear—every day. It is just assumed that the weather will be a constant.

What happens when the weather is taken off the table? What happens when we don't have to think about it? We might be able to eliminate a lot of mental weight, shedding the burden of having it hang over our heads all day every day. A single outfit per day. One wardrobe instead of several seasonal ones. Less stuff—no umbrellas, rain jackets, snow pants, or winter boots to haul out or put away.

In our creative practices, we can take the weather off the table. It is a world that is our own, designed for ourselves. There are things that we can choose to keep off the table.

Eliminating Possibilities

When it comes to quilting, there are countless techniques we can use—from traditional piecing to improvisation to foundation paper piecing to hand piecing to bojagi—and that's just piecing fabrics together. For the actual quilting part, we have hand quilting, chunky hand stitch, tying, straight line, free motion, domestic machine, long-arm quilting. Our choices of material are infinite: solids, modern prints, naturally dyed fabrics, linen, cotton, recycled, digitally printed, vintage, polyester thread, metallic thread, cotton thread, recycled thread. And there is a pattern for every taste and occasion.

It's a very big quilting world indeed. There are so many possibilities and so much potential waiting for us. It's a petrifying feeling, being faced with boundless opportunities when staring at a blank canvas or a blank page. Where do I even begin?

Guess what? You've already begun. You've eliminated all[1] the other creative media out there. You have chosen quilting. And now that you've made that choice, let's zoom in. What else can we eliminate?

---

[1] I say this to make a point, but the truth is, I personally like all the creative media: quilting, ink drawing, digital drawing, calligraphy, watercolour, animation, music, and the list goes on. I've chosen quilting to be my main one—the one I often use as a lens through which to see other media. For those of you who can't always choose, I see you.

- Experimenting with different techniques lets you discover what you don't like. Cross it off.
- Is there something you don't want to spend time learning (yet)? Free motion quilting, for example, feels daunting, and you don't have the time to learn something new, so take it off the table.
- Is there something you don't have the equipment to do (yet)? Off the list.
- Is there something you don't want to make the time for right now? English paper piecing, for example, allows us to make intricate and amazing designs, but it is labour-intensive. Put it aside for now.

Now, we don't have to deal with this or that unknown and the weight that it brings; it's been eliminated.

This corner that we've found ourselves in—it's not limiting; rather, it's freeing. It unburdens us from the weight of constantly considering all possibilities. Every time you take a possibility away, you make a choice— a positive choice to allow you to move forward. You've eliminated the chaos of the weather.

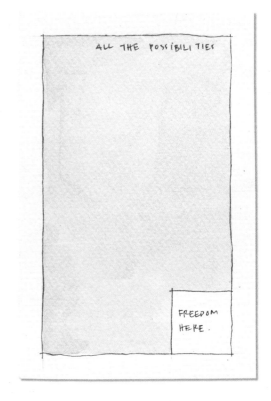

Eliminating possibilities gives us freedom.

CHAOS #2: Untamed Land (Natural Topography)

Not far from where I live, about an hour's drive down the southern shore of Nova Scotia, there is a small town named Lunenberg. It is a picturesque tourist destination with houses and buildings in every colour of the rainbow. If you were to imagine a quaint east coast town, it would look exactly like Lunenburg. Founded in 1753, Old Town Lunenburg is today a UNESCO World Heritage site. As a shining example of eighteenth-century British colonial settlement in North America, its rectangular grid pattern of streets and wooden vernacular architecture give it "Outstanding Universal Value"—a UNESCO term used to describe its heritage significance. The town is built on a hill, and when you view it from across the harbour, you can see its

Lunenburg, Nova Scotia, as seen from the deck of the *Bluenose II*. Photo credit: Kim Werker.

colourful buildings cascading down toward the water. It's truly a sight to behold.

I put myself in the shoes of a colonial bureaucrat in charge of planning this new settlement. I strive to make this wild land a prosperous place for myself and for my settlers. I impose some logic onto this "untamed" land.[2] At this point in history, the city grid system is already millennia-old and the basis for many great cities around the world—tried, tested, and true. A grid can be efficiently built. The residents will understand how the streets are organized. Everyone will get a small, but equal parcel of land.

As a quilter, grids are how I organize my world. Unit by unit and block by block, I build something that becomes a cohesive whole. As the modules repeat, they give me a sense of rhythm: temporally, as I make them; and then visually, when the blocks come together to make a quilt top. New York City is a dream for many reasons, one of them being I can never get lost walking around because of its grid system. My preferred kind of notebook page to organize my thoughts, lists, and projects is a dotted grid. I can navigate myself in two dimensions in orthographic relationship. I deeply get grids and grids get me.

Lunenburg's town plan based on a grid seems logical to me; that is, until I have to walk up one of its cute streets from the harbour. It goes straight up that beautiful steep hill. Even the streets that are parallel to the water span two hills, so I'm walking down and up a rollercoaster to get from one end to the other. The elevation difference between the harbourfront and the top of the two hills is about forty metres—roughly ten storeys— over a few short blocks. I am almost certain that whoever planned this town had never actually set foot on the land and experienced its topography.

---

2   I put this in quotes because the land was inhabited before the British settled there—first by the Mi'kmaq and then a small number of French Acadian settlers, who co-existed peacefully before the British expelled the Acadians from this region.

Respect the Topography

The wild landscape of our lives can be tamed when we impose structure onto it. Schedules provide us with modules of time to work within. Units of production give us a sense of yield: responding to emails one by one, writing a paragraph at a time, striking tasks off a to-do list, learning from a series of online quilting workshops. But these grid-like structures, while logical and efficient, may not always be the best way to make creative progress with enjoyment. It can feel like an uphill battle or an artificial city grid forced on a unique topography.

I am not an avid hiker or a particularly active person, but a few years ago, I visited Banff National Park embedded in the Canadian Rockies. I spent several hours hiking up, and then down, a mountain. If you've ever hiked a trail in a mountainous region, you may understand a better way to get up a steep incline is to follow a series of switchbacks. These are paths that have gentler slopes, almost parallel to the shape of the hill, that gently zigzag upwards. They can seem slower and less efficient than going straight up the side of a mountain, but they provide a way up that reduces the amount of resistance. A longer path, but less daunting, more doable, and more enjoyable for more people.

We can run into unproductive resistance[3] in our quilting because we sometimes ignore the distinctive quirks of our minds, personalities, and bodies. A creative practice has a natural topography; I think we should be considerate of it.

The natural curvatures of creative practice are unique to each individual:

- A tendency toward a scale of working: tiny scraps, king-sized quilts, or something in between.
- A time of day that is conducive to creative output: early morning, afternoon, or late at night.
- A persistent question that requires many experiments.
- A specific technique that sustains our interest and asks us for a long-term deep dive.
- A pattern of quickly moving interests.

Then there are things that are immovable objects in our landscapes—circumstances in a particular moment or a chronic reality:

- An elderly family member that needs to be visited regularly and be taken to appointments.
- A toddler that wakes frequently at night.
- A health issue that causes back pain.
- A neurodivergent brain that works beautifully, but defies conventional order.
- Grief that comes in unexpected waves.

In our creative practices, we can take the weather off the table, but there are some conditions that we need to accept and work with and around. These topographies and landscapes help us form our unique interests and ways of working.

---

3 Resistance is only bad when there is no hope of getting through it.

CHAOS #3: Grief and Pain (Immovable Circumstances)

A few years ago, I worked on a collaborative quilt with visitors to a public museum. I met hundreds of people from different parts of the country and all over the world. Whenever a child came by my work area and showed interest in the fabrics I was working with or my sewing machine, I gave them some fabric scraps to take home as a little souvenir in hopes of inspiring them when they got home. Many months after the quilt was finished, I received a message from a dad of one of the families that stopped by. He and his wife had gone through a painful separation shortly after their family vacation when they had visited the museum. During that time, he decided to make a couple of blankets for his kids to express his care and love for them. He had never worked with fabric before. In delving into working with textiles, he told me, he had found a way to sort through his own grief and emotions. He found it therapeutic to work with his hands while processing his own pain. He wanted to thank me, because he had included the fabric that I had given his children in his creations for them.

Many of us find solace in quilting, textiles, or fibre. Life's pains—personal illness, a stressful job, a broken relationship, caregiving, loss of a loved one, a global pandemic—are inevitable, but a creative practice gives us a temporary way out. It gives us a breather.

For a few minutes, we can escape into a world of quilt math and colour selection; we can get lost in rote tasks like chain piecing or pressing fabrics. Then we can take a deep breath before returning to the reality of a heavy situation. And a creative practice doesn't just give us a moment to breathe, it also gives us space to make a way through.

Filling a Space to Make a Space

When I busy my hands, it fills up a small void in my psyche. It's like repairing a drafty window: When the draft is no longer disturbing the air, there is stillness. Making things with our hands quiets the air so we can process heavy emotions. I can pray or meditate with, oddly, less distraction. I can allow my emotions to flow while my hands are at work. Maybe I prefer the feeling of being productive even with small simple tasks, rather than wallowing in nothingness (which is also an important and legitimate way to feel grief or pain). By making time to create with my hands, my mind can be more present to work through difficult things.

We can take the weather off the table. We can work along our natural tendencies. We can work through those immovable parts.

A SOFT PLACE TO LAND

> *When people think of quilts, they think about warmth and security. So they can be a kind of soft landing—a way to tell the story of difficult topics.*

—DR. CAROLYN L. MAZLOOMI, Historian, Curator and Artist,
Founder of the Women of Color Quilters Network (WCQN),
2014 National Heritage Fellow, National Endowment for the Arts

Dr. Mazloomi's idea is that quilts provide a space for us to confront difficult subjects, particularly injustice and racism. As she puts it, "Every human being in the world has a 'cradle to grave' relationship with textiles." Quilts are familiar; they are a source of comfort. They are closest to our vulnerable selves—our precious babies, our bodies while they slumber, our homes.

The idea of a "soft landing" can cast a very wide net. Cutting fabric and stitching it together provides a safe place for any idea to be investigated, meditated upon, confronted, and birthed into something else. This can be on a personal and individual level; it can be external things like illness, relationships, and loss, or internal things like contradictions within ourselves, restlessness, and renewal. As in Dr. Mazloomi's case, the soft landing can also be a way to confront societal ills, collective grief, and systemic failures. You might think that some stitched cloth cannot make change, but it mostly certainly can—even in the smallest of ways. It can invite someone into a challenging conversation without threat or defensiveness.

DESIGNING A CREATIVE PRACTICE IN A DISORDERED WORLD

I've mentioned that I approach everything as a design problem. A design or creative brief is a document that lays out constraints and parameters around a problem that needs to be solved. We are essentially going to do that for our creative practice. But before we go about looking at those helpful limits, we need to agree on a core belief about the nature of creativity.

Expressing creativity seems like a privilege; it could sit comfortably outside our basic needs. However, to me it is not a luxury; it is a way of being. The history of quilting tells us that no matter our economic reality, the state of our health, or our place on the hierarchy of societal power—there is a way to make quilts. If this is the way we accept it to be, we can build a creative practice from that tenet. We can design a way of being within our given circumstances that includes quilting.

Our lives have demands on our time, space, money, and energy. We have a limited amount of these four resources, so realistically, how we distribute them is mostly not out of choice. These immovable circumstances are things in our lives that we can't choose, but we accept. Our quilting practice is bound to and rooted in our everyday reality in this way.

Budgeting Our Resources

Let's explore some questions about how we can spend our resources on quilting, which will give rise to the shape of our quilting practice. I use the word "spend" with intention.

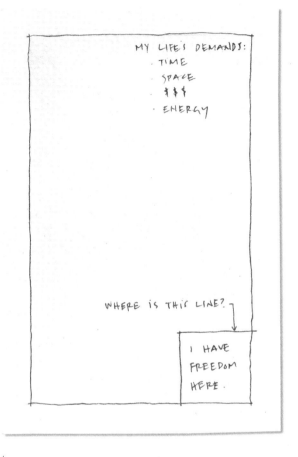

The boundary of our creative practices takes our resources into account.

In our young parenthood days, my husband and I created a line in our monthly household budget called "Andrea Projects." The amount was somewhere in the range of two or three medium-fancy coffees. We also assigned Sunday afternoons as a time when I would wander out of our apartment to do whatever I pleased. Often, I would end up at our local fabric store, sometimes renting a machine for an hour. If I thought maybe I would skip my Sunday alone time, my husband would basically push me out the door. It was essential—the designated spending of funds and time—for me to get through the other 165 hours of the week spent with an irrational toddler while being pregnant.

I could ask, "How much can I *give* to my creative practice?" instead of "How much can I *spend* on my creative practice?" Giving is usually seen as over-and-above, outside of necessity, special and out of the ordinary. Spending, on the other hand, is inside the realm of necessity, a fact of life, everyday and very ordinary. I don't consider feeding my children a gift. I simply spend the money at the grocery store, because I have a responsibility to nourish and care for them. To spend is to rise to a responsibility; I have to do this creative thing for our lives to work.

The spending questions we ask have to do with the four resources of time, money, space, and energy:

Time. How much time do I have (per day or per week)? This can be as little as ten minutes before you get ready for the day or a block of three hours each weekend. A regular rhythm that works for you will help you form a habit and commit time to your creative practice.

Money. How much money can I spend on quilting (per week or per month)? The cost of a fat quarter is similar to that of a latte. Finding second-hand or thrifted fabrics can be as thrilling as shopping for new fabric. The amount and type of fabric can help determine the size and type of project that will best suit your budget. A quilted clothing item or bag will use less fabric than a bed quilt. A hand-stitched project will have you using up fabric at a slower pace, so the need to purchase new supplies will slow down as well.

Space. How much space do I have to work? You may have a guest bedroom dedicated as your sewing space or you may have a small desk in your living room. You may only have temporary use of a corner of the dining table and you have to set up your machine and put it away every time you sew. When setting up and tearing down is a necessary element of your time, ensure that the amount of setup time is proportionally appropriate to your time spent cutting fabric or sewing. If it takes you fifteen minutes to set up and put things away and you have thirty minutes for your daily sewing time, it might be worth the effort to sew for one-and-a-half hours, twice a week, to make the most of the time you have between set up and tear down.

Tidying your space is also part of your practice. This is one that I struggle with because I don't want to "waste" my precious creative time with cleaning up. However, clearing up physical space keeps the feeling of overwhelm at bay and helps me think more clearly about the task at hand. I tend to do a good clean after a forefront project is complete, even if I have multiple projects going on at once. Tidying is not wasted time; it can allow you to focus better or work more efficiently on a particular task. The stage of your project can also have input here: Some people work better in messier spaces, where they can see a lot of things at once. I find this to be true when I am in an inspiration/design phase, but less so in a production and execution phase.

Energy. How much energy or brain power can I spend on my creative practice? This may mean physical energy or mental energy. If you're too tired at the end of the day to sew, then perhaps first thing in the morning might serve you better. Or an end-of-workday/pre-supper time slot. If you're in an especially mentally taxing period (e.g., report card time for a teacher, tax season for an accountant, waiting on a medical diagnosis), then maybe it's the right time for an easy pattern or quilt kit, where you don't have to make many choices or learn a new skill.

Once we have established the bounds of these four resources, we commit to them. The answers to these questions alleviate us from making these decisions on a day-to-day basis, which takes up time and energy. We can succumb to decision fatigue, where it becomes impossible to make creative decisions because we have poured ourselves instead into making mundane decisions of when and where and how much. I find it easier to decide ahead of time, and only once, and then make a habit of it, as opposed to making the decision daily around whatever else is going on that particular day. Designing a creative practice is akin to meal planning: Do the planning and shopping once a week, then all the recipes and ingredients are ready to go. No decisions need to be made. It is freeing.

Designing an intentional practice also helps us avoid making decisions—particularly bad ones—on a whim. It holds us accountable. When you're at your local fabric shop, it's helpful to know what your budget is before you step foot in the store. If we don't feel

like sewing during our allotted time, we may just need a little push to show up because enjoyment comes once we start. There is room for whim within our creative practice, but it doesn't help us to establish the structure of one.

Your decisions about how to allocate your four resources, as well as considerations of the various external and internal chaotic forces in your life, should allow you to see the shape of your quilting practice and how it fits into your life. Work within these bounds for at least a little while, until you see that something outside has changed or something within doesn't quite work. If you find that the way you've designed your practice is not conducive to the way you want to create or the way you want to live, then it's time to revisit these questions. If it becomes more restricting than freeing, we return to the drawing board and make big changes or small tweaks.

Having a creative practice means that we can design it. Designing it means we have choices. And having choices means we are empowered. ✕

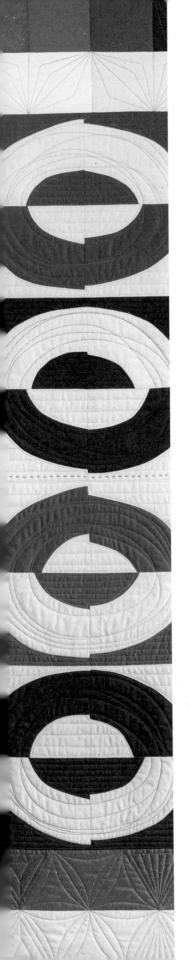

Essay No. 2
Building Containers

I enjoy listening to podcasts. A good portion of my time is spent solo in my studio, busying my hands with the work of making.[1] I put on my headphones, constructing for myself a little portable room with its mental door closed. I move about from my sewing machine to the ironing station to the cutting table and back. Podcasts give a linear and progressive sense of time to the rhythmic and repetitive nature of preparing fabrics, making a series of quilt blocks, or binding a quilt. Having an audio window into other people's ideas, stories, and worlds gives me a grounding sense of being a part of a bigger world, especially because I'm in my own head a lot of the time.

Several years ago, I came across Oprah's podcast and in particular, an interview with Brené Brown—a professor who has spent decades researching courage, vulnerability, shame, and empathy. She vaulted to fame with her top-five TED talk entitled, "The Power of Vulnerability." Today, one of the things she does is help organizations apply her research to the way they lead in whatever context they find themselves. In her book *Dare to Lead*, Brown talks about building a safe container: "Building a safe container is the process of

---

1   Don't be fooled; most of my artist's life is not spent creating art. Most of my time is spent at the computer writing emails, doing administrative tasks, sitting in meetings with mostly interesting people, coordinating projects, and writing proposals of one sort or another. But I try to make something with my hands daily as part of my workday.

establishing the ground rules of a group—what rules need to be in place for people to feel safe to communicate and to freely express their ideas and concerns. Taking the time to create a safe container builds trust and improves communication. It provides an atmosphere where team members can be vulnerable and take risks."

As a self-employed artist, I don't work for an organization. I am not a hospital administrator that needs to work with hundreds of different contractors, I do not own a multimillion-dollar business with several employees, I do not run a non-profit that takes in injured wild animals and nurses them back to health, nor am I a teacher who manages a classroom so that my students will learn well. But I do see my art practice as a mini organization where I am both employer and employee. I cast a vision for my art practice and lead myself toward that vision. I set up learning spaces for myself. I create ways for me to grow. I am the administrator of my organization. Thinking about it this way keeps me moving along with a sense of direction and purpose.

When I apply the idea of building a safe container to my mini organization/practice, I make small adaptions to Brené Brown's description:

> Building a safe container in personal creative practice is the process of establishing the ground rules or constraints, for me to feel safe to communicate and to freely express my ideas and concerns. Taking the time to create a safe container builds self-trust and allows for self-reflection. It provides

an atmosphere where I can be vulnerable and take risks.

Within my creative practice, I build containers where I can ask questions: my whats and hows and what-ifs. I carve out a little safe space with these questions—a small amount of fabric, a small amount of time, a limited number in series. The outcomes are sometimes small explorations that end up as cast-offs, sometimes larger projects with larger investments of time and material and bigger risks, and sometimes it's simply knowing how it feels to go through a process.

From Quilt Show to Quilt Blocks as Containers

If you've ever had the pleasure of attending a quilt show, it is a trove of mind-blowing inspiration. At every turn, breath is taken away, curiosity is piqued, and emotions are stirred as we connect with the work and the maker. Even so, the experience can also be overwhelming because we are constantly putting ourselves in the position of the quilter. "How did they make that?" "Could I make that, too?"

When I see breathtaking improvised works by masters like Sherri Lynn Wood, Sheila Frampton Cooper, or Émilie Trahan, I feel sense of awe and inspiration. I might think to myself, "I would like to give that a try someday." And then the thought sits in the back of my mind for a while. It can be daunting to surrender a whole quilt to a completely new way of working, with no guarantee of favourable results. So how do I enter this uncharted territory?

Awaken
2021
50" × 64" (127 cm × 163 cm)
Quilted by Sheri Lund, Violet Quilts

One of my favourite quilts that I have designed is my *Awaken* quilt pattern. This graphic quilt depicts daybreak, the awakening after night's darkness—a new beginning with each new dawn. When I conceived of it, I wanted to be able to give people (myself included) a taste of improv piecing within *safe containers*—discreet and manageable rectangular blocks arranged within a familiar grid.[2] Because of the improvised piecing, there is variation amongst the blocks, but they are set in an orderly fashion and against the breathing room of negative space.

As we see what sort of things we can squeeze out of this notion of safe containers, we're going to rummage through the tickle trunk and try on few different hats: researcher, novelist, and teacher.

CONTAINER #1: The Research Lab

Young children have an exhausting penchant for asking countless questions. Sometimes their questions make us notice how much knowledge we take for granted as adults. "Why is water wet?" "What is infinity?" Sometimes their questions make us wonder alongside them. "I don't know the answer to that question, actually." Their curiosity is refreshingly delightful—on a full night's sleep, that is. The number of questions that children ask actually begins to decline when they start going to school.

The Reggio Emilia Approach® is a philosophy of early childhood education developed by Loris Malaguzzi and parents from an Italian community (named Reggio Emilia) in the post-World War II era. One of the key underpinnings of this approach is the assumption that children are *researchers*. They construct knowledge by asking questions that interest them, building on what they already know, exploring answers and solutions through projects in a community setting. If you look at today's scientific research methods, they look a great deal like the Reggio Emilia Approach. I have taken on this way of thinking and being in many areas of my own life—from the way I interact with my children to the way I cook, to the way I orient myself in my creative practice. In my quilting, one example of such "research" has to do with experimenting with line.

I learned to draw and sketch in university at architecture school. We were required to spend two hours a week, for many semesters, freehand drawing human models. In parallel, in the design studio, we learned how to draft—first by hand, using pencil, and then with ink. In the following years, we added computer drafting and 3D computer modelling to our arsenal of design tools. I tended to sketch and model in analog, turn to the computer to refine ideas, then return to drawing by hand for my final drawings. When ink is applied to

---

2   This approach to improv may have subconsciously flowed from my first introduction to improv, a workshop called "Speed Dating with Improv" with quilter and teacher, Krista Hennebury of Poppyprint.

paper, there is a sense of finality—decisions are made that cannot be retracted, only worked around. Seemingly infinite rounds of design iterations come to a head and there is little you can do but move forward. I love that feeling of forward momentum.

In the decades that have passed since then, I have not made any amazing pen drawings or developed my skill to any notable level. But pen and paper have continued to be a mainstay in how I think and work out ideas, whether it is through written notes in my bullet journal, cursory sketches of quilt designs, or a 100-day project that involved a brush pen and index cards. For the last few years, a question has stemmed from my relationship with this medium and has sustained my interest: "How can the act of line drawing be interpreted in fabric?"

From this point of curiosity and over the period of a few years, I have done a lot of testing within projects to see where it will go. The studio has become a research lab, a place to ask questions and search for answers.

What is it? How will it work?

In my research lab, a safe container can take many forms: What can a quilt block look like if I only use blues from my scrap bin? What improv technique works in this limited six-inch-by-eight-inch block? What might it be like to make a quilt out of Tyvek (a fabric-like building material)?

One such instance stemmed from this doodle and sketch in my notebook (page 35). I became preoccupied with how this image might be brought to life in fabric. Curiosity was sparked. And what ensued was a Pandora's box of questions as I explored and discovered.

What is it?

- Is a line printed, is it a stitch line, is it a bias strip, is it pieced?
- Will the lines be "coloured" in? Or will the lines sit on top of a single piece of fabric, like a wholecloth quilt, like a drawn line on a page?

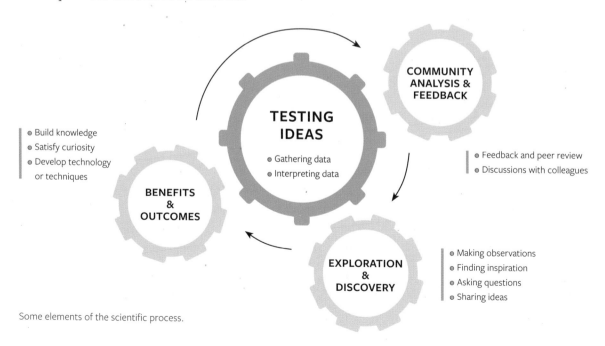

- Build knowledge
- Satisfy curiosity
- Develop technology or techniques

BENEFITS & OUTCOMES

TESTING IDEAS
- Gathering data
- Interpreting data

COMMUNITY ANALYSIS & FEEDBACK

- Feedback and peer review
- Discussions with colleagues

EXPLORATION & DISCOVERY

- Making observations
- Finding inspiration
- Asking questions
- Sharing ideas

Some elements of the scientific process.

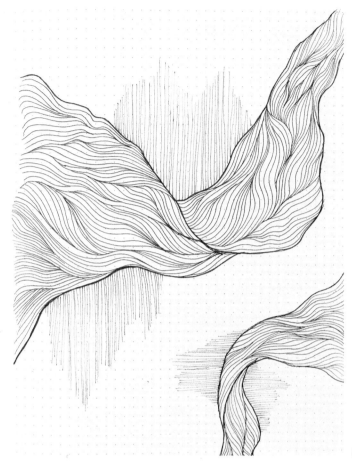

Line drawing from Andrea's notebook, 2019.

- How will the different weights of the lines be rendered? Wider and skinnier strips of fabrics? Different weights of thread?

How will it work?

- What type of materials will I need?
- Do I need any special equipment?
- Can I quilt through these layers?
- Who can I ask that might have experience working this way?

Each of these small questions is a container to test within. We can set up experiments with an acceptable, usually small, amount of investment of time and material. We go in with a hypothesis: These materials, equipment, and processes can achieve what

I want. The first thing I did was ask another artist, Emily Watts, who had worked with bias tape appliqué and linework before, how she approached it. She was so generous in sharing her own "research findings" (what worked and what didn't, which kind of machine worked the best for her, what she had explored and hadn't explored). I wanted to build from this knowledge and see if it could be applied to my own drawing.

A couple of years after I had made that initial drawing in my sketchbook, I had a larger commission to work on that pushed me to embark on answering many of these questions about line. The project was a collaboration with curator and artist David Woods, who

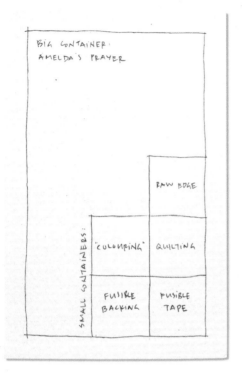

Amelda's Prayer as a big container to investigate a variety of questions relating to "line."

works with African Nova Scotian quilters to turn his sketches about rural life in the province's Black communities into large-scale quilts for a collection and exhibition entitled Secret Codes. David's initial sketch for *Amelda's Prayer* had these ethereal swaths of colour behind the foreground figure (image 7, page 37). I imagined my line drawing—but with colour—as this background. *Amelda's Prayer* became a big container to hold several experiments together, and to accomplish it, I made many smaller containers to build up toward it.

One of my first tests was with off-the-shelf fusible bias tape over sections of colour, fused on a background. Disappointingly, the fabric puckered. There is nothing more dismaying to me than puckered fabric; the perfectly flat

colour in my mind and computer renderings (another one of my safe containers!) ended up all wrinkly and shadowed. It didn't work the way I had hoped it would; my hypothesis had been refuted. I then asked for advice from another friend and guildmate, Gillian Noonan. She suggested another stiff fusible and so I continued to iterate from there. Each time we try something new, we collect new data—what works and doesn't, whether we like the process or not, what results are favourable and which aren't quite there yet. A quantity-over-quality attitude inside the container can be beneficial in order to gather the right data.

The aim is to test in a low-stakes, controlled environment, so when the time comes to take a bigger risk, we have a base level of certainty that it will work. Just like researchers in a science lab, we can isolate questions and seek answers before applying them to the larger world. So before we make that bigger quilt or a quilt intended for submission to a quilt show or exhibition, we can figure out the what and the how. A technique can be developed in a safe container and subsequently applied to a general creative practice.

Over time, I sought out answers to my specific questions in service of the bigger question about line and fabric—with different pieces at different scales and different end uses. Some started as test blocks and remained tests and nothing else. Some are commissioned works that have hung in quilt shows, exhibitions, or homes. Some are in limbo and might someday become other things. The benefits and outcomes of my research have been to satisfy my curiosity and to develop a method that works for my future intentions.

IN FABRIC, A LINE CAN BE:

… printed [1]

… stitched [2]

… a bias strip adhered to another
surface [8]

… pieced [3]

- Will it be "coloured" in? [4]
- Or lines on top of a single piece
  of fabric, like a wholecloth
  quilt? [5]
- How will the different weights
  of the lines be rendered?
- Wider and skinner strips of
  fabrics? Different weights of
  thread? [2]
- Who can I ask that might have
  some experience working this
  way? [6]

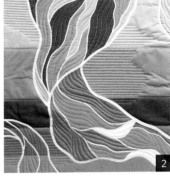

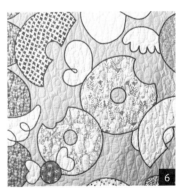

1 Andrea's design hand printed by Alissa Kloet,
   Keephouse, 2020
2 *Red Earth, Interrupted*, 2022
3 Test, 2023
4 A section of *Quiet & Roar*, 2022
5 A still life composition, 2021
6 A section of *Radioactive Flying Donuts*,
   by Emily Watts, 2022
   53" × 70" (135 cm × 178 cm)
   Quilted by Sarah Campbell
   Photo credit: Emily Watts
7 Original sketch by David Woods
8 *Amelda's Prayer*, 2023
   51" × 70" (130 cm × 178 cm)

CONTAINER #2: The Fictional Plane

As evidenced by my high consumption of interview-form podcasts, stories of real people are of endless fascination for me. I thrive on hearing and learning from other people's experiences. They often inspire me and spark a creative response. History, traditional quilt patterns, and real quilts made by real people whom I will never meet, have all been starting points for me in my own creative work. For a person who is so taken with narrative, though, it may surprise you that I only recently started reading fiction.

I am an extremely slow reader. I also nod off easily within a page or two of getting settled in to read comfortably. This unfortunate combination has made it difficult for me to enjoy books. Up until the recent past, I read when it was required of me: for school, for research, for learning something new. One day in the depths of a pre-pandemic winter, my sister lent me a book that held my interest—nothing taxing or earth-shattering, a rom-com type novel. I didn't need to read it on a timeline, nor was there any expectation that I would have any "takeaways" from it. I could read a page or two—or more—a day and it wouldn't matter. It was merely good entertainment, like a fluffy-yet-satisfying movie, only many hours longer and therefore providing a larger quantity of entertainment.

As I meandered my way through more fiction in the subsequent years, I realized what I had been missing out on: the opportunity to try on different people's perspectives and experiences, however fantastical and unrealistic the setting or situation—to feel what they feel, ask the questions they ask, wonder the same wonderings, and then see how their actions and reactions might play out. Proponents of the arts in education, and in particular theatre education, emphasize the way imaginary worlds provide this kind of pathway toward developing empathy: the creation of a fictional space that is a non-judgmental space to be yourself or try on other selves, with little at risk. When you delve into these stories, nobody actually dies, but you can experience a character's grief. Nobody actually becomes a TV star, but you can go on a character's journey from yearning to actualization. No one actually falls victim to an epic heist, but you can relate to the team of thieves' sense of camaraderie.

How will it feel?

When we build containers for ourselves in our creative practices, we can feel safe to try on something new and different and see how it feels. We make a little bubble for ourselves with no audience to perform for. Like an artist's sketchbook whose pages are reserved for only their own eyes. We can be vulnerable, take risks, and possibly experience:

- fear
- failure
- joy
- doubt
- satisfaction
- disdain for a process or technique
- delight
- rejection

- courage
- frustration
- relaxation

An example might be that you have this big idea that you want to make a memory quilt for your child out of their old baby clothes. How might you feel about cutting into their clothes? How might you feel about working with the range of different types of fabric?

A container for this big idea might be to choose the least sentimental piece of clothing that you have saved and make a simple quilt block out of it—a nine-patch or a sawtooth star. If it's not a simple woven cotton, even better; two experiments can be rolled into one. Do the research into what interfacing might be best to apply to the fabric. Make the block, perhaps mixing in scraps of quilting cotton from your stash. How does it feel? Are you ok with "messing up" the clothing? Do you mind preparing and mixing the substrates?

If it is not an enjoyable experience, is it possibly worth it to work through your displeasure in service of the big idea?

When we pre-approve the risk and accept the cost, the more negative experiences are mitigated, to a degree. We lose a preset amount of fabric which is now unusable and we invest a preset amount of time with no tangible outcome. When those negative feelings arise, we build resilience by setting out another safe container to try it again in a different way. Maybe the next container for the quilt is to change the design of the quilt block, or maybe the conclusion is that you would rather commission someone else with more expertise in making this type of quilt to do it for or with you.

Just like in that fictional book, nobody has actually died. Our containers are safe spaces with ground rules that we have set, to catch us when we fall, or to help pick ourselves up when we do.

CONTAINER #3: The Classroom

My mother is a retired teacher and she spent the last decade of her career teaching the littlest ones in their first year of public school. Their chubby cheeks, baby teeth, little lisps, searching for the right words to describe their unadulterated thoughts, needing help with their jacket zippers at recess time—they were her very favourite age group to teach, so open and innocent. She cared for them and they knew it. They'd accidentally call her "mom" on a regular basis, as young children tend to slip up when speaking casually to

a consistent and caring adult presence.

But Mrs. Tsang was not the kindergarten teacher that you might imagine—the archetypical woman that was especially warm, gentle, and maternal. That is *not* her. She is quite straightforward, verging on blunt. "No, Abigail, you cannot be a princess when you grow up," she would say matter-of-factly. "But what else could you imagine yourself to be?" She set out clear, and high, expectations for these tiny youngsters. Given the right kind of attention, help, work, grit, sometimes a few tears—for which she was present every step of the way—her expectations were attainable. They would take pride in their work and so would she. She was firm in the belief that they were all capable and unique individuals and they trusted her to take them on a journey of learning. Some of these littles were reading by the time the school year's end rolled around. There was no curricular requirement for them to be able to read, but they could and they were off on their own journeys of discovering and understanding the world through their newfound literacy.

How will I get there?

Teachers create a setting for their students in order for them to learn well. They say, "Here's where we're headed!," point the way, set up steps for them to get there, and accompany them on the journey.

Teachers are there to "scaffold," to provide temporary supports that help build up knowledge and ability until they are no longer needed. The imagery of construction scaffolding makes it quite clear; if you've seen any buildings undergoing maintenance or repair from the exterior, a modular metal tube structure is built to allow workers and materials to fix hard-to-access heights and areas. (As a young adult, I visited Hong Kong and noticed how different their scaffolding looked—it is constructed with bamboo and nylon ties.)

Our safe containers are scaffolding for us to learn something new. Scaffolding in our creative practice can look like:

- Breaking up an idea, question, or technique into chunks, like I did with my line explorations. With each chunk, find tools and structures to help.
- Building on prior knowledge. What do you already know about it? How can you build on that knowledge? If something is completely new or far outside your ordinary way of working, then you can make sure your learning is broken into very small chunks—baby steps.
- Providing opportunities for multiple attempts, such as repetitive exercises to practice a particular technique.
- Giving yourself positive reinforcement. There may not be an external person around to tell you you're on the right track like a teacher, so you will need to step back from what you're doing and see what's working and what's not. For me, I can tell I'm onto something when I feel a sense of satisfaction.

Once you feel like you can comfortably and competently wander outside your safe container, you have unlocked something. The safe container, or in this sense, the scaffolding, is no longer needed. The test block is no longer needed and you can dive into the real thing.

What is the new thing I want to try?

(e.g., improv patchwork curve, a single embroidery technique,
a new material or a new medium, poetry in textiles)?

What do I need to know first and whom can I consult?

THE CONTAINER

Size limit

Colour or colours

Time limit per repetition

How many times will I repeat this?

Any other constraints I want to put
on this new thing?

REFLECTION

◎ What did I enjoy about this?

◎ What did I not enjoy about this?

◎ Do I like the results I have
produced?

◎ What specific elements do I like
or dislike? Why?

◎ Should I try this again with any
changes in material, process,
colour? If yes, when?

A THING OR A WAY

In the safe containers that we build for ourselves, we can ask questions and take risks. In the research lab, we can ask, "What will it be? How will it work?" In the fictional space, we can ask, "How will it feel?" And in the classroom, we can ask, "How will I get there?"

Once the container has been explored, we can go about our creative practice with something new in our toolbox. For a results-oriented person like me, I easily tend to look for some *thing* to come of it. For example, a series of improvised blocks that was a creative exercise will become a quilt. But just as valuable, or even more so, is coming away with a process-oriented learning—the outcome is a *way*. A way to think, a technique to use, a method to explore further, an understanding of how we derive joy and satisfaction in our creative practice. ⚒

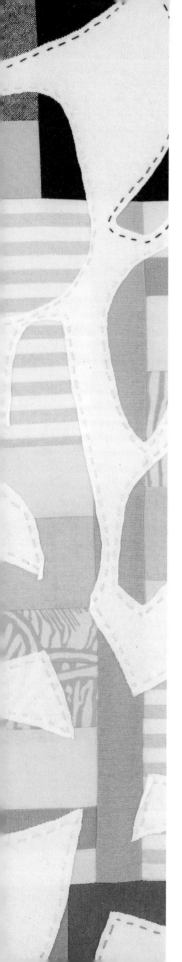

Essay No. 3

Surrender

Our musings thus far have taken what life has given to us—all its chaos, unpredictability, and responsibility—and within it, carved out a deliberate or contrived space for ourselves to create. Inside that space, we design safe containers for ourselves: measured and controlled experiments that add or revise our databases of knowledge about our craft and ourselves. These can be seemingly heavy-handed manipulations of our time, resources, and energy in service of building a creative practice. For me though, planning and designing is naturally the way I go about the world; it's a grooved path that my mind follows with ease. What doesn't come as comfortably is surrendering to a material or process.

On one end of the spectrum of surrender is the lightness of spontaneity, whimsy, and play. What if we allow ourselves to do it for fun and without consequence, just because we want to? The spectrum's other end is more contemplative and brooding: the unknown, mystery, and fear. What if we allow ourselves to do it even if we don't know how, what the outcome will be, or how it will feel? These are not the baby steps within our carefully designed safe containers, but rather bigger leaps that may not turn out to be just for-my-eyes-only inside-my-sketchbook flops, but major[1] public failures.

---

1   When I say "major," I do want to highlight that, with some perspective, most of them aren't actually major; they just may feel that way in the moment. Nobody's life is totally dependent on the public success of your creative practice.

In her book *The Rise*, author Sarah Lewis delves into the story of polar explorer Ben Saunders. In 2003, Saunders made a 240-kilometre ski trek (about 150 miles) to the North Pole—by himself; this was after an already failed attempt. Almost a decade later, he would take a nearly 3,000-kilometre expedition (about 1,795 miles) with a partner to the South Pole. He describes himself as a craftsman or artist, one who tests the boundaries and endeavours to discover; and when confronted with human limits in his arduous journey that he may not complete, he does not resist the wind, temperature, or his physical pain. He uses the word *surrender* for that "wonderful" feeling. Lewis writes:

"Surrender...might be an imperfect way to describe it. The term with the white-flag retreat of loss in the context of battle. Yet when feelings of failure come with their own form of pain, empowerment through accepting it—surrenders—and pivoting out of it can be more powerful than fighting." p. 70-71.

Our creative practices are spaces where we can surrender, where we can let go, giving ourselves room to listen and be open in the expanse of the unknown, to be fuelled by something we didn't even know existed.

FORCES

I have already painted a picture of the weather conditions in my part of the world that govern my everyday activities and behaviours. When I moved to the east coast after spending most of thirty years living in Central Canada (Ontario and Québec), I brought with me all my assumptions about a rainy coastal climate. Winters are quite grey, it's often drizzly and foggy, and it's a bit unpredictable. Shortly after I arrived, I bought a sturdy and stylish umbrella, the kind that is a bit of an investment for an accessory but is justified because of its anticipated frequency of use. But nobody told me about the sheer irrelevance of the contraption that is an umbrella when gale-force winds are part of the raininess on a regular basis.

There's a photo floating around the internet, showing a crunchy Cheeto embedded in a broken lock, acting as a comically poor replacement for the hardware needed to keep a door shut and secured. It has taken on a life of its own as the basis for several memes like, "Username: Admin, Password: Admin" and "When you try to contain your laughter in serious situations." One such meme says something like, "An umbrella in an Atlantic storm." Thanks to such forceful winds, rain falls toward my body at a horizontal. Not only did this umbrella not protect me from getting wet, but my good, sturdy, expensive umbrella would either flip inside out or threaten to take me away like Mary Poppins.

Here's the thing about the wind: It's not out to get me. It's not trying to make my life harder. It just is. But it is its force that I sometimes have to contend with.

One of the largest forces that paralyzes us is the unknown. We can build ourselves safe containers and work within those to figure out some things, but other things are simply not knowable. Let's look at the example of submitting a quilt to a national quilt show. We can't know how many quilts will compete in a given year; we can't know what this year's judges are particularly interested in; we can't know what other quilts are in the categories we enter. It's a bit mysterious and a bit subjective. But one thing that is not a secret: It's not about *you*—the judges and the show organizers aren't personally trying to boost your ego or tear you down. These things we can't know aren't, for the most part, nefarious.

When we recognize what is the limit of our knowledge, we can surrender to that boundary. We can sit more comfortably without knowing. We can consciously act out of acceptance of those limits, instead of defaulting to inaction because we can't know. What's beyond that limit can't dominate us.

Surrender, in a lighter sense, is the possibility for creative play and spontaneity. We can make what we want, just because. In the words of my wise colleague Cheryl Arkison, "It doesn't have to *be* anything."

I am of two minds. Part of me is extremely pragmatic and strategic; what I make has to be useful or moving toward something. The other part of me knows that there is more to it than what I can see, plan, or strategize. The creativity inside us can be accessed by messing around, noodling about, and meandering. Happy accidents happen when we do this—

a colour combination speaks to us, or the way one shape meets another sparks a new thought. Why not increase the chances of these occurrences by playing around more?

This book—so far—has mainly addressed an individual type of creativity, but the longer I lean into my creative practice, the more I am convinced that "creative energy" lies not only inside us, but that it exists somewhere outside ourselves. *Transcendent* is too a strong word, but there is a creative ethos that lives in the world that we can take hold of and run with.

In her book *Big Magic,* Elizabeth Gilbert shares a story about a time when she started a novel set in the Amazon and then put it aside for a while. She believes that she passed it on to her fellow author and acquaintance Ann Patchett when they met for the first time in New York City—at a panel discussion about libraries—via a greeting kiss. When they chatted again in subsequent years, Ann told Elizabeth that she was working on a novel with the very same, very specific settings with the same specific plot line. Elizabeth had never spoken to Ann about her previous work. The notion that she passed this idea to Ann is somewhat believable if you can believe that the idea lay outside either of them begin with.[2]

Not only does creative inspiration tap individuals on the shoulder, but it can be part of a collective subconscious. It has happened in science, math, and engineering as well. The same research is conducted in different regions of a pre-digital world; this is referred to as "multiple independent discovery."

I was recently on a jury to evaluate artist

---

2 The novel became *State of Wonder,* by Ann Patchett (Harper, 2011).

proposals, and several included projects to do with mushrooms. None of the artists were working together; none of them were in the same medium. Then I noticed that mushroom fabric seemed to have popped up in just about every fabric manufacturer's lookbooks in the last couple of years. There is a collective wondering about the magical powers of mushrooms to open up psychedelic worlds and journeys of healing. The fascination with mushrooms is not completely new, but it's been renewed. There is just something in the air; questions that are longing to be investigated in a particular period.

When we meet these creative prompts in the world, we have a choice: to ignore or to listen.

When confronted with the unknown, we have a choice: to resist or to accept with an open hand.

RESISTANCE

Before I frame *surrender* in the context of our brain's reactions to threat and fear, let's remember how living a creative life greatly matters and how it doesn't matter at all. It matters for us to be curious, present, and enlivened through creative practice. It's better for ourselves, the people around us, and for the world, that you are the best version of yourself because you have a place to express your creativity. But we are not necessarily solving the world's problems and certainly no one's life is at stake.

Our brains, when presented with a threat or a feeling of fear, have four common automatic responses: fight, flight, freeze, or fawn. There are physiological responses stemming from the amygdala, the part of the brain that perceives fear, which sends signals to the hypothalamus which in turn activates your nervous system. The body releases adrenalin and cortisol which can affect your heart rate, breathing, pupil dilation, hearing, skin, and pain perception. These are all physical symptoms triggered by a psychological fear. From these physical responses, our bodies go into these subconscious modes—fighting back, running away, being paralyzed, or appeasing the threat.

In creative practice, we may be presented with situations that scare us. They are not urgent or life-threatening, but they can require some courage to face: submitting a quilt into a show or an exhibition, trying a new technique, joining a new quilt guild, acting on a flash of inspiration. We can tackle an idea to the ground and wrestle with it. We can tell ourselves we can't handle it and flee. In the context of creativity, the most common form of resistance is freeze—inaction. If we hold the view that acting on creativity is luxurious and superfluous to our existence, then it's easy to let it pass us by.

× × ×

Sand is a funny thing. I once saw a science exhibit where you could look at samples of sand from different regions under a microscope, and they are essentially tiny rocks—like a collection of mini-rocks representing all the minerals that can be found in that region: quartz, granite, sandstone, et cetera. The minuscule size of each grain allows it to act like a liquid while not being wet. You can pour it; it will fill every crevice it is allowed to access.

If you grab a handful of dry sand and wrap your fingers tightly around it, some sand will fall out. Gripping it too tightly limits the amount you can hold. A fistful of sand is constrained by its tight enclosure; it resists the natural properties of the sand. However, if you cup your hand with your fingers gently held together, you can receive a mound of sand. In addition, the most sand you can hold is when you have both hands open together and someone else gives it to you.

Struggling with hard things can be like gripping sand. We fight them so hard that we spend all our energy battling, with little left to invest in our creative pursuit. Receiving creative energy can be like holding sand. A loose but careful hold. It is being open and listening.

OPENNESS: Magic and Mystery

One late-March morning, I arrive at the airport to catch a small daily flight to the remote town of Gander, Newfoundland—of *Come from Away* fame. As I approach my gate, I scan the crowd for a person that I have not ever met in real life, only in the two-dimensional world of virtual meetups over the last three years. I find her bright smile in a crowd of mostly men destined for offshore and mining work. She—Ranee Lee of Toronto—and I are headed off on an adventure to Fogo Island. It was a quilt that brought us together and to this place.

In January 2020, shortly before the world shut down because of COVID-19, fellow quilt artist Libs Elliott and I mounted an exhibition in Toronto's Regent Park neighbourhood as part of the DesignTO Festival. DesignTO is an annual city-wide celebration of design in all its forms. Exhibitions, window displays, talks, symposia, parties about interior design, user experience (UX) design, architecture, graphics, interdisciplinary work—the city is alight with activity in the deadest of winter months. Our exhibit was titled *FACETS*, stemming from the multi-faceted gemstones I had been exploring for a few years, but also the facets that give meaning and richness to human life.

In preparation for the exhibition, I finally tended to a seed of an idea that had been nagging at the back of my mind: the new architecture of a small community in the North Atlantic, one of the "four corners of the Flat Earth" according to lore, Fogo Island. This island, a ferry ride away from Gander, has a rich history of fishing, before the cod stocks were depleted in the 1990s and the economy collapsed. Through the radical vision of one woman, Zita Cobb, and

Opposite:
Fogo
2019
40" × 50" (102 cm × 127 cm)
Photo credit Ranee Lee

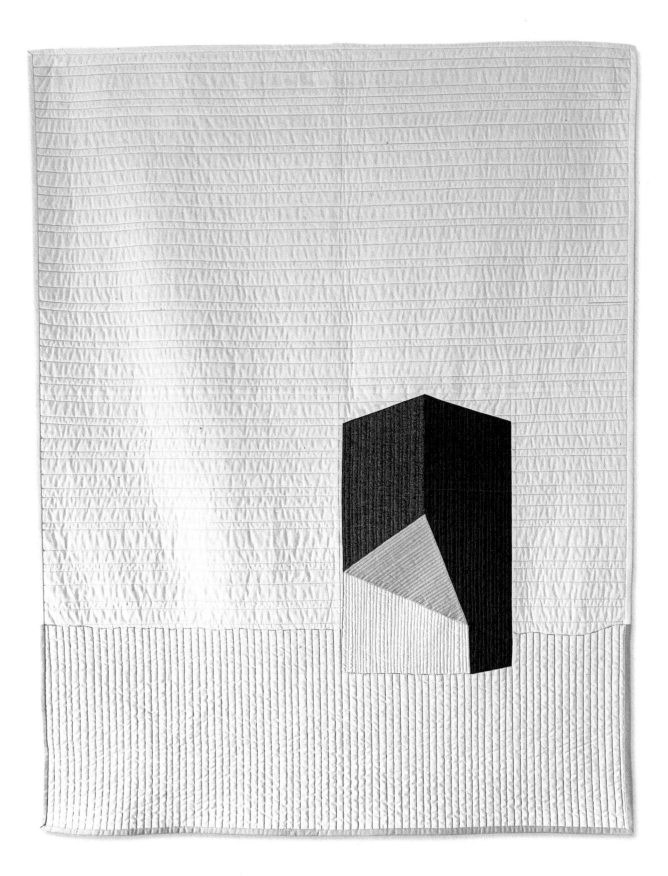

her generous—and arduous—long-term investment of funds, energy, community consultation, and more, the island's economy was revived through tourism, architecture, art and design, craftsmanship, and community development deeply rooted in place. The contemporary architecture of a very special inn, as well as four artist residency studios, were designed by Newfoundland-born, Norway-based architect Todd Saunders. The studios themselves are quite extreme shapes, capitalizing on the rugged and unique landscapes that surround each. This place was on my (quite short) bucket list of places to visit. The faceted forms held such stark beauty and because of my interest in geometric forms, I really thought a quilt should exist to interpret them.

So I took the Regent Park exhibition as an opportunity to do just that. I only managed to create a quilt of one of the four studios, which was a simplification of the landscape and form. I long-arm quilted it myself in a very minimal style, honouring the way the building is clad and having it "rise" out of the landscape. Libs and I hung our quilts for the week-long festival and after the festival's opening, I left Toronto to come home.

A few days after I came home, I got a message from someone who had seen the quilt on display in Regent Park. She was interested in purchasing the quilt called *Fogo*. The message was from Ranee Lee, an industrial designer who taught at the OCAD University in Toronto. It turns out she had had a very long research interest in Fogo Island and its unique approach to community development. Moreover, she had been working with a sewing collective of women, most of them immigrants, located in Regent Park and had been aiming to help them find a way to become economically sustainable. The merging of textiles and Fogo at this very location sparked her to inquire about the quilt; it seemed it was made specifically for her.

We met virtually every few months over the following years, first to get to know one another—we had a startling number of things in common: our ethnicity, our sports-loving boys, our worldviews, our love of good design, and our penchant for anything black-and-white. The conversation turned quickly to the possibility of collaboration. It was a bit vague and nebulous, "there's a connection here; there is potential here...." At one of our meetings three years in, she told me, "So—I'm going to Fogo in three weeks...do you want to come with me?"

Our adventure was filled with magic and surprise. The time of year that we found ourselves there, I would have never planned for myself—pack ice season, between winter and spring, where the ocean is filled with constantly moving shards of salty ice that bring seals down from the Arctic. The people that we met: another traveller from Washington, D.C., whose decades-long filmmaking career and life story were lessons upon lessons to draw from; locals that were among the most warm and welcoming people we'd ever met; the architect himself who was there at the same time; the unexpected sunshine and calm winds; the makers of the quilts on our beds while visiting around the community; the artist at the Gander airport on the way home, who felt like a kindred spirit.

Since our trip, Ranee and I have, in fact, done some concrete things together: running virtual and in-person workshops and an exhibition, and, as always, there's the possibility of something else down the line. Showing up to meet with a stranger-become-friend time and time again for no substantive reason or tangible agenda, and nurturing a sort of mysterious connection—this is what surrender can look like. It's holding our hands open and keeping our eyes open to what is unknown. The unknown doesn't have to be scary or nefarious; it can be a new friend and a new adventure.

My seed of an idea was a quilt depicting an artist studio in the far reaches of Newfoundland. What is a seed of an idea that you have been carrying around that needs to be planted?

SURRENDER TO MATERIAL

One of the things I struggle most with as a designer is the difference between the theoretical and physical reality. Digital tools in design have made things quick and easy to mock up before we make the real thing. This is a safe container for me—a digital space to test out ideas with just time and no materials as my investment. As a person who tends to use solid colours in their work, translating a solid flat digital colour into fabric often brings about disappointment. How come this fabric isn't flat? Why is this seam not straight? Why won't it lay completely flat? And especially, why does quilting have to ruin my perfect design?

I often say to myself, "If I worked in a hard medium like wood, things would be easier. I could get my design to look the way I want it to with crisp edges and neat, tidy joins; the wood would do what I want it to do." This is, in fact, a lie. Wood's properties make it do unruly things like warp, bend, and swell. Knots and imperfections add to its misbehaviour, as does the humidity in the surrounding environment. Different kinds of wood behave differently; putting one next to another adds yet another layer of complexity.

"I'm trying to create something here; I have a vision to execute. Can't you just behave and do what I tell you?" I say to the fabric. We tend to try to control and dominate the medium; that's why we use starch and every tool conceivable. The medium is there to serve my purposes, right? This inclination is something that my mentor, textile artist Frances Dorsey, pointed out to me. "Fabric is fluid; it moves," she said. "You can't always control it." Or "Why don't you leave that edge raw?" she would say. And my modern quilting sensibility would kick in and I would recoil.

All materials have their unique quirks, which can bring about frustration and tension. But we don't have to tame them. We can get to know them and work cooperatively with them, and then they can sing a song in harmony with you as the creator. I dare say that I think this is what a craftsperson does: They work in concert with their material. They have a closeness and intimacy with their medium.

SURRENDER TO PROCESS

A few years ago, I began work on a project to make new art pieces inspired by old quilts in the Nova Scotia Museum collection. There was one particular double wedding ring quilt in impeccable condition from 1943. Its scrappy rings were appliquéd by hand onto a white background with a heavy black blanket stitch. I thought, "Wouldn't it be wonderful to bring a discarded wedding dress back to life by cutting it up and putting it back together in the form of a double wedding ring quilt? Wouldn't it be poetic to turn an imaginary sad story of a discarded wedding dress into something beautiful?" Off to the thrift store I went, arms linked with a thrifter friend, and I soon found a couple of dresses to work with: one with silk crepe and a silk lining from a well-known label, and another with polyester lace, a polyester lining, and modest shoulder pads. Together, these two dresses provided a nice variety of opacities and textures of fabric—they were "scrappy" even though they were all shades of white.

The big question became, how to piece these wildly different fabrics, some of them quite slinky, together. After a few tests and consultations, I landed on applying a dissolvable adhesive stabilizer to normalize the stiffness of the fabrics across the range, then proceeded to cutting and piecing. The very *last* step of the process, once the double wedding ring was pieced and then appliquéd by hand to a silk organza background, was to dunk the entire thing into water to rid it of the stabilizer. This was *after* I had done the hours of work to get to that point. It was a bit of a

From top:
Wedding dresses. | Appliquéing the pieced double wedding ring to the sheer background. | Dunking.

terrifying moment, plunging all that work into a vat of water, swishing it around in hopes that all the stitches would stay and that all the raw edges I had left intentionally wouldn't fray the fabric into oblivion.

I pulled it out of the vat, gently squeezed out some of the water, and laid it in the sun. I waited for it to dry. Hours passed. When it was fully dry, I examined it. It looked wrinkly—ethereal—like I imagined it, but not perfectly flat and resolved. I wasn't dismayed, but I wasn't thrilled. When I see the piece now, I don't see the wrinkles as much. I see a process, not a final product. I see an internal process and a material process that I had to surrender to. I think of that dunking as a moment of surrender which gave me an opening, a measure of bravery that I didn't know I had. I can return to that moment and know that I can let go and surrender to yet-unproven outcomes.

Redemption, 2020. 31 ½" × 36" (80 cm × 90 cm).

PIVOTING OUT

When explorer Ben Saunders talks about the pain of failure, he talks about empowerment through accepting that failure and that "pivoting out of it can be more powerful than fighting." What are some ways that we can be more open-handed and accepting in our quilting practices, but also in life? Here are some prompts that set you up for potential small failures within your quilting practice and then branching outward beyond it. If it goes poorly, ask yourself, "How do I pivot out?"

- Make a quilt block with a fabric other than quilting cotton.
- Use your ugliest fabric or least favourite colour in a quilt block or project.
- Denyse Schmidt, sometimes called the "mother of modern quilting," has had her students put fabric scraps in a paper bag. She then asks them to pull two out and sew them together. Try it. Then pull out another piece and add it to what you have. No peeking as you draw from the bag!
  - Pull out leftovers and forgotten condiments from your fridge and see how they can be combined into a meal.
  - Similarly, pull out forgotten items from your wardrobe and see how they

can be combined with your current favourites for a new outfit.

- *Still Life* (page 92) invites a lot of blind acceptance of a process. Reading through the stages of the process, there are a few moments in the project where you are given an "out." Where would you get off the train?
- Make a quilt block using scissors instead of a rotary cutter. Or use a rotary cutter but no ruler.
  - Try baking something without a recipe. Maybe start with something you've made before and do it from memory and add a new ingredient.
  - Look for connections between quilts and a random item, place, or person. Some examples could be: a quilt and a lettuce leaf, a quilt and Antarctica, a quilt and Beyoncé.
- Look for connections between two people in your circles that have very little in common.
- If you've never been to a quilt show, find one near you to attend. There, you will find people that are open and also be exposed to many kinds of quilts.
- Say "Isn't this quilt magnificent?" to a stranger at the show, as you both admire the same work.
  - Similarly, say "Hi, how are you?" to a stranger in your community and be genuinely interested in their answer. Someone who you are already interacting with, like the person serving you a coffee or ringing in your groceries, is a prime target.

What might pivoting out look like? With a quilt project gone awry, it could be stepping away for a period before returning to it. This may lead to a decision to lean into it or to walk away from it. It can be turning it into a small project, like a tote bag, and giving it away. I would like to encourage you to stick with it for one or two more steps beyond what feels comfortable, before discarding the experiment. The spirit of "pivoting out" does not mean "getting out of it," but rather it means find a creative way around it. This creative tenacity is not forceful; it is walking a path of wilful surrender.

When it comes to surrender, the main questions to ponder are:

- What part of your quilting process do you hang on to most tightly? How can you let it go?
- When things don't go as planned, how can you "pivot out" rather than walk away?
- How do you live a more open-handed life? ✕

Essay No. 4

Responsibility to Self

Somebody may have told you in your youth that you are special. I hope that someone has told you that in your adulthood, too. It's true—we each have a unique combination of nature, experiences, opinions, relationships that makes us, *us*. Only you can be you. And you are responsible for making that happen.

"To thine own self be true." A quick Etsy search finds this inspirational quote emblazoned on every type of product you can imagine—posters, nursery wall art, coins, pendants and charms, graduation rings. It is Shakespeare's *Hamlet* that offers us this ubiquitous aphorism—a line in a speech by Polonius (a bit of a shady character in the play) as he sends his son on his way to university. These words of wisdom, regardless of the virtue of their speaker, have stood the test of four centuries: Being true to yourself is still an aspiration held in very high esteem in our contemporary Western context. A twenty-first-century version might be, "Be authentic" or "You do you."

But who is "thine own self"? Who is this "you" that you must remain true to? And what does it have to do with quilting and creative practice? There are several things that make me, *me*. Some of it resides inside me, some of it lies outside me, some of it is what I aspire to. These "Circles of You" are different parts of us that make our life unique: how we are wired intrinsically, the circumstances that surround us, and our aspirations. Once you have laid out what your circles are, you can begin to define your personal mission in your creative practice, address some of the things that prevent you from moving toward achieving that, and become comfortable enough with yourself to look at your own work with a healthy, critical eye.

THE CIRCLES OF YOU

The Unique You

When I was a teenager, I loved flipping through teenybopper magazines and finding fun and silly quizzes to do: "What shade of lipstick are you?" "What type of friend are you?" "Who's your celebrity match?" I never took them very seriously and yet I enjoyed taking in those datapoints and seeing if they could give me insight into myself. It makes sense that at that age, I was looking for ways I could fit into the world. I think that search never really ends; we're always looking for a way to "fit" and belong, especially as we grow and change, our circumstances change, and the world changes around us.

But there are some things about us that don't change greatly over time. There are many personality tests out there, much more "serious" than my dear quizzes from *Seventeen* magazine: Myers-Briggs, StrengthsFinder, the Enneagram, to name just a few. Other systems, such as tests based on Howard Gardner's Multiple Intelligences theory, uncover how we learn and solve problems. Over the years, and in different contexts, I've gone through these frameworks. I've learned a lot of descriptors for the way I am and behave, and by contrast or similarity, how other people around me are and behave: emotive, stoic, rational, instinctive, introverted, analytical, adventure-seeking, peacemaking, image-conscious, outgoing, suspicious, fair, connected, detail-oriented. None of these attributes are virtuous or bad, in and of themselves; they could be either in any given situation.

I find this knowledge of myself helps me map the natural topography of my interior workings, "mine own self." Here are some questions to get you thinking about the way that you are: What motivates you? What gives you satisfaction? How do you relate to people? How do you naturally approach problem-solving? What brings out the bcst and the worst in you?

Your Unique Life

Our life circumstances are an amalgam of choices that we've made and things that are beyond our control. Some of the choices we make have consequences that we can't plan for. In the section *Order in Chaos*, we've already acknowledged that there are circumstances in our lives that are beyond our control—immoveable objects in our landscapes that we must design our creative lives around.

What is true of all these circumstances is that they build your experiences, help form your outlook, inform what you think about and the way you work creatively—they make you uniquely *you*.

You probably don't need a lot of prompting to understand what these circumstances and choices are in your own life, but here are some possibilities.

- Your financial circumstances, both as a child and as an adult
- Where you live, which could have been a choice or could have been where family or a job led you

- Commute times
- Access to a diversity of people
- Access to a diversity of experiences
- Living in rural or urban settings
- Whether you are the primary caregiver for another person, older or younger than you
- Physical health challenges
- A neurodivergent brain
- Having kids
- Having a kid that is going through a major transition period, such as a baby's sleep regressions or teenage angst
- Having a kid with special needs
- Grief, a very old one or a very new one
- A rewarding but demanding job
- A job that is not in an area of passion for you

Your Unique Life Goals

I don't know if I had grand dreams for myself when I was growing up. The question, "What do you want to be when you grow up?" had a different answer every year of my childhood. A teacher, a writer, a doctor, a nurse. As an adult, I now know that we never really arrive at "growing up." Our jobs, the responsibilities in our personal lives and communities...they're always changing, expanding, and maybe even contracting. Instead of, "What do you want to be?" the question might be, "What is important to you?"

Maybe it's providing a comfortable and stable physical and emotional environment for your family, maybe it's travelling the world, maybe it's travelling to your country of origin, maybe it's a priority for you to experience really tasty food, maybe it's important that you be physically fit. Perhaps there are career

ambitions that you have, or you want a certain work-life ratio. Maybe you want to be able to work from anywhere. Maybe you want to make an impact in your community—whether that's organizing your quilt guild's next social event, volunteering at the food bank, or serving on a board of a local non-profit.

These aspirations might overlap with your creativity or they could be quite separate. For me, one of my broad goals is to continually find creative fulfillment and to build a career around it. For someone else, expressing creativity might be outside of the job that pays their bills.

In any of these cases, your unique life goals orient your life in a certain way, and you will spend your resources on these things as a matter of sculpting a life that you want.

Your Unique Creative Aspirations

At this point, we have established that creativity is important to you, and that expressing and developing it is a priority.

Within the realm of your creative practice, there are likely goals you have in mind. You may want to:

- Deep dive into and master a certain technique or set of techniques
- Master a technique to be able to teach someone else—a young quilter or a seasoned quilter wanting to expand their knowledge
- Learn as many techniques as possible, from painting and printing on fabric to hand piecing
- Find your own artistic voice
- Find friends through the shared passion of quilting
- Spread the joy of quilting
- Spread love by providing and coordinating community quilts
- Use the medium to explore certain questions or express specific ideas (e.g., social justice, a specific colour combination)
- Earn some income
- Find solace and expression during a difficult time
- Just have fun

The things we want to get out of our creative practices are so varied. If you're like me, many of the points on this list resonate—I want to do it *all*. But I only have twenty-four hours in a day like you, so how can I be intentional about the time that I spend on my quilting endeavours?

YOUR CREATIVE MISSION

In the chapter *Building Containers*, I talked about leading yourself like you were an organization. One of the practical ways that can play out is envisioning a future you would like for yourself and then writing a mission statement for yourself to work toward it. Businesses and organizations have this type of statement to help them focus on what matters to them. It informs choices about how to allocate resources like time, energy, and finances. In a creative practice, it is an internal compass—it gives me purpose and I can be intentional about what I focus on. Within a couple of years of starting 3rd Story

Workshop, I came up with a three-pronged mission: To let people know what quilting is today; to help people along in their creative journeys; to elevate the domestic arts.

A mission statement does not have to be made public. The mission can be just a few notes you jot down in your notebook and come back to every so often. It does not have to be static; it can evolve with time, as you shift and the world around us turns. In the years that have passed since I wrote that initial mission statement, the art world has shifted to be more open to textiles and domestic arts as comparable to other traditional art forms such as painting and sculpture. The work is indeed not finished for them to be considered equal, but there has been movement. It may not be as important to me in my practice to push this conversation anymore, because I see that being fulfilled by other artists and in other spaces. I have begun shifting that point to a more specific mission to push domestic arts into the public realm.

The Circles of You—The Unique You, Your Unique Life, Your Unique Life Goals, and Your Unique Creative Aspirations—determine the shape of your unique quilting practice at this moment in time and deliberately orient you toward a future that you would like for yourself. They make connections from your inner self and past self to your present self to your future self.

BARRIERS: The Three-Headed Dog

Now that we've thought about your unique quilting practice and maybe even articulated a mission statement, let's address some of the things that might prevent you from moving forward or following through.

Cerberus is a minor mythological creature that you may have never heard of—a three-headed dog from Greek mythology who guarded the gates of Hades so that the dead would not be able to leave the Underworld. A more well-known version of this beast is the character Fluffy from *Harry Potter and the Philosopher's Stone*, by J. K. Rowling. Fluffy is also a menacing three-headed canine, who guards a trap door which leads to a hidden treasure. If you know how the story goes, he can be subdued by the sound of music. He falls asleep at the sound of any melody and keeps slumbering so long as the music continues playing.

Fluffy is a metaphor for the things that keep us from quilting. You may have noticed that a Fluffy often sits in front of your sewing room or studio door, keeping you out. Let's name this Fluffy's three heads and learn the melodies that will keep him asleep.

Luxury

"I have more important things to do right now." As mentioned previously, expressing creativity can seem like a privilege, beyond the necessities of life. There will always be dishes to do, underwear to fold, another email to write. There are always necessary things to do and some of them are most definitely important to do in a timely manner.

If I use this fifteen minutes to sew up a simple quilt block, will I regret not using that time to do a sink full of dishes? It's possible that it will make my life less fun tomorrow. But at the end of your life, will you have regretted that sink full of dishes? Probably not. Or maybe it's not even an either/or. "I will take the last thirty minutes of my day to do the dishes and sew up a quilt block." We can build it in.

Melody #1: Necessity.
Creating is just as important to me as exercising, getting outside, having good sleep habits, eating well. It is nourishment.

Quality

"I won't make anything good today." "My idea isn't original enough." "I will just be wasting time and material on an outcome that won't be good or of any significance." If you're waiting for your chance to make one perfect thing, I am here to tell you that I know it will come while you make one hundred imperfect things. Quantity will lead quality.

There is a famed parable in creative circles, recounted in David Bayles and Ted Orland's book *Art & Fear*, in which, on the first day of a ceramics class a professor announced that students would be divided into two groups. One group would be graded solely on the quantity of work they produce, in this case, clay pots. The other group would only need to produce one perfect pot to get an A. At the end of the term, the "quantity" group produced the best work, freely experimenting and learning from their mistakes. The "quality" group *thought* a lot about making the perfect pot but had little to show for their efforts when it wasn't executed well in their one pot. If you make a good number of things, you will eventually make something good.

Melody #2: Acceptance.
The aim is showing up and making; just doing it. The aim is not perfection.

Potential

"I'll get to it someday." The maybes and somedays of creative work prevent us from going through the door. "When I'm retired." "When this other phase of life is done." "When there is more time." There is a time for creative thoughts to exist inside our heads, but there is also a time for them to come out and be realized.

I was at my son's middle school recently, and in the music room there are inspirational quotes posted everywhere. One that caught my eye said this: "A goal without a plan is just a wish."[1]

Melody #3: Realization.
My dreams of a creative life are here in this present moment.

Fluffy, is a tameable creature. The tunes we play in our head can put him to sleep so we can do the creative work we are trying to do.

You are responsible *for* yourself and you are responsible *to* yourself. You are the boss and you are the underling. These are ways you can do that: Knowing "thine own self," accepting your present circumstances, actively pursuing what you aspire to (however minuscule the steps you take), separating yourself from the thing you've birthed so you can look at it with new eyes.

---

1   The phrase, which had no attribution on the poster, is from *The Little Prince*, by Antoine de St-Exupéry, a children's book chock-full of wisdom. A sewing room with a collectible stash, the best machines and gadgets—even a simple desk with a machine in the corner of your living room—is merely potential. It's a wish for something. To act on the potential, there needs to be concrete steps to make the making happen. It can start with a commitment to showing up.

RECLAIMING CRITIQUE

The voices in our heads can be loud, the negative ones especially. "I failed high school math so I could never design a quilt." "These points aren't coming together perfectly; I must not be a very good quilter." The inner critic, for some of us, is a dominant force in our minds and can dictate a lot of our actions. It limits what we can think we can do. And for that reason self-criticism can be a dirty word.

However, I want to suggest that *critique* is a positive thing that can propel us forward, rather than hold us back. The key difference between self-critique and self-criticism is a separation between our work and ourselves. If we can hold the work outside ourselves, if we can put some space between who we are and the thing we create, then a negative comment doesn't become an attack on us as a person, but just the work. It's easier said than done, because creative work is often so deeply personal. Our self-worth can be easily wrapped up in the product we make, but it's in the making that we discover ourselves; that's where the worth lies—in ourselves.

A good teacher will do the same with their students; they help their students see that the work they do is separate from their value as a person. The quality of the work may be a B-minus on some grading scale, but doing the work and grading the work is only a mechanism for feedback. In service of learning, the teacher offers constructive feedback so that the student might progress and apply the lessons learned to the next attempt.

I am happy to report that in our creative practices, we get no grades. Nobody is tasked with marking you.[2] There is safety in our creative practice, because we are not compelled to show anybody the work. It can be completely private, if we so choose.[3] You are called to the role of teacher, in charge of your progress, if that is indeed one of your goals. Self-critique is very contained: you, yourself, and your work. Do you like it? Are you satisfied with it? What parts would you change? Is it possible to change it?

You step outside the work as the maker and look at it from various outside angles. Take on different perspectives: another quilter taking it in at a quilt show, or a gift recipient. You can take those thoughts into consideration or, alternatively, discard them outright.

Let's not treat critique as nefarious. It is not out to get us and beat us down. It can serve a good purpose. ✕

---

2 Unless you're paying them to be your teacher or a judge—for example, in the academy or in a juried show. And then it is a choice you consciously step into.

3 This is a perk of a personal creative practice—it is a shelter you build for yourself. You can hide inside it as a place of refuge, or you can invite as many people into it as you desire. My experience has been that our worlds become bigger when you let others in, to share your work, build trust, and share feedback. It taps into the *collective power* of quilting, which I address in the next chapter. And then it is a choice you consciously step into.

Essay No. 5
Collective Power

I have an acquaintance who is a painter. She's been painting since her early teenage years and was something of a prodigy—think Oprah interviews, numerous appearances on American national television, and a reference to her remarkable abilities in a child psychology textbook. In recent years, Amanda has turned to quilting as a new-to-her mode of expression. She said something in one of our conversations that has stuck with me: "Artists in other media don't do this...this free-flowing exchange of knowledge and passion between creators. Quilting is unique in that way."

Being steeped in the quilting world, we may not notice this uniqueness. I remember that feeling of embrace[1] when I first joined a quilt guild. People were interested in what I was creating, they were invested in encouraging me throughout my process, and genuinely desired for me to pursue quilting in whatever way was true to me. This strong sense of community was striking to me, as it was to my painter friend. Quilting is rarely an individual pursuit; it is done with other people.

The community aspect of quilting has been evident for centuries. In America, during the late eighteenth century, farmstead activities—such as barn raising, harvesting, and quilting—brought communities together. These types of activities were both necessary and fun: Necessary for keeping families

---

1   This may not be everyone's experience in the quilting world—it can certainly be cold and exclusionary, as any group of people can be.

warm in the cold winters, but also an excuse to gather in a social setting. Quilting, as with much textile work, was the domain of women.

By the late nineteenth century, hand-crafted industry—including quilting—became part of social reform movements, aimed at providing employment to the poor. These cooperatives were jointly owned small businesses that produced goods and were operated by their members for mutual benefit.[2] What is it about this art form and craft that makes it this way? What is this collective spirit that seems inherent to quilting? Some hints can be found in the history of guilds, the existence of folk art, the rise of women's voices, the meaning of monuments, and the use of modular technology.

THE BACKSTORY ON CRAFT GUILDS

In the Western world, the notion of craft guilds goes back centuries, with their roots in growing urban populations in Europe between the eleventh and sixteenth centuries. The pre-industrial era required many craftspeople, usually men, to produce everyday goods—hat makers, carpenters, bakers, blacksmiths, weavers, and masons. Merchant guilds also existed alongside craft guilds, where membership was made up of all merchants involved with regional and long-distance trade in a town or city. Reasons for forming guilds were multifold: economic interest, apprenticeship, standards of quality, specialization, and mutual aid.

Economic Interest. Guilds could essentially form a local monopoly on their goods, limiting supply and control and regulating the prices of their products. Guilds were able to band together and fight for legislation that would favour their membership, especially merchant guilds.

Apprenticeship. Guilds could educate and train people into their craft professions using a system of apprenticeship—starting with apprentices who earned no money but were provided room and board; moving up to journeymen who made daily wages; and onto master craftsmen, who could be business owners.

Standards of Quality. Setting and enforcing quality standards on the products made by guild members reflected well on the profession and the guild as a whole.

Specialization. Because guilds existed in higher population areas, the opportunity arose to specialize in specific skills of the craft. For example, for efficiency and to capitalize on expertise, a masonry guild could have a specific member focus primarily on making mortar while others focused their efforts on brick laying. This division of labour increased profit margins and meant better quality products.

2 "Cooperatives," World Quilts: The American Story, International Quilt Museum, accessed August 14, 2024, https://worldquilts.quiltstudy.org/americanstory/creativity/cooperatives

Mutual Aid. Members took care of one another in times of need, paying for burials and dowries for the poorer families. During the fourteenth-century bubonic plague called the Black Death, for example, guild members and their families became family units in themselves, supporting each other as death swept through.

Craft guilds from this time period diminished with the dawn of industrialization, and the need for craftspeople declined sharply in sixteenth-century Europe.

North American quilt guilds as we know them today were formed during the 1970s, possibly as the result of several coincidental events: A 1971 landmark exhibition, *Abstract Design in American Quilts*, at the Whitney Museum of American Art; a key 1972 article in *Life* magazine about the quilting cooperatives that had cropped up in the 1960s in relation to the civil rights movement; and the nostalgia of the American bicentennial in 1976 that had people looking back at past traditions.

Most of today's quilt guilds are less economically and professionally driven, but as the craft guilds of centuries prior did, they provide many learning opportunities—both informally amongst guild members and by bringing in speakers and workshop teachers to expand the knowledge base of their membership. They are often structured as non-profits with elected officers and membership dues, and they often function to promote the craft to the wider community. Other trade-focused organizations, such as Studio Art Quilt Associates (SAQA) and the Craft Industry Alliance, provide economic and professional resources for artists and business owners in the quilting industry.

QUILTS AS FOLK ART

When my kids were young, I took a few years away from my work in the design world. During this time, I made a handful of quilts, two of them for my kids. I found it satisfying—as I always did—to make something with my hands, but even more so to have a respite from taking care of an infant and a toddler, day in and day out. Once my kids were of preschool age, I wanted to ease myself back into working again and quilt pattern design seemed like a fun way to use my design skills. After making a handful of quilts, I joined my local modern quilting guild to see what my potential customers would be like. And there, I found a world.

Quilt pattern design, art quilts, improv quilts, traditional quilts, fabric of every colour and design, solids and prints. Craft shows, craft exhibitions, fine craft galleries, art galleries, craft business, quilt industry. There was a lot to take in.

I had decided very early on that my design sense was very modern—using exclusively solid fabrics. There was a certain minimalism in the way that I worked, echoes of my design training in architecture school. Geometric shapes, angular forms, similarities to graphic design, straight line quilting. I knew these attributes aligned with the going definition of modern quilting.

But outside of the quilting world, what was it? Having not gone to art school, thoughts about where my work "fit" confused me. I obsessed over this. Was it art? Was it fine art? Was it design? Was it craft? Fine craft? "Crafts"? And then, most perplexing: Was it folk art?

At the time, in the mid 2010s, whenever I looked for quilts in museums, they were most often displayed in folk art museums, not art galleries. For me, the term "folk art" conjures up the image of a maritime fisherman spending his onshore winter days whittling spoons out of driftwood by flickering firelight. Their whimsical sardine-shaped handles are carved improvisationally, then painted in bold primary colours. Our most beloved folk artist in Nova Scotia is Maud Lewis, a painter who sold her "primitive" and "child-like" works at the side of the road for mere dollars. Now her works are held in our provincial art gallery's collection and in the private collectors' market, the original paintings can go for tens of thousands of dollars. There have even been forgeries made and sold.

Most definitions of folk art highlight the artists' lack of formal training in academic settings—using terms like "self-taught," "traditional," "decorative," and "utilitarian." Another frequently mentioned aspect of folk art is the reflection of a culture or community rather than individual expression of ideas. Often the learning of the art form happens amongst community members. You can see how something like folk music fits all these descriptions: Someone learns to play the fiddle from their grandfather; they play, sing, and dance at community *ceilidhs* (pronounced "kay-lee," Scottish Gaelic for "kitchen party"); and the cultural tradition gets passed from generation to generation. Nobody in the family has taken formal lessons at a conservatory and the music is not performed on a stage—its utility lies in its expression in a community setting. My quilts checked every box according to these definitions: self-taught, rooted in centuries-old tradition, learned from peers in my local guild, utilitarian, decorative, reflective of a community or culture.

One of our biggest culture setters and a place for community is social media— Instagram, TikTok, YouTube, and before these, Flickr. These are places where you can learn to quilt, develop skills, and exchange ideas and thoughts about quilting. I learned a few things from early YouTube videos before social media was such a ubiquitous part of everyday life. These spaces give rise to a "collective ethos" that is also driven partly by the market—what fabrics are popular, colour palettes that are having a favourable moment, a nostalgia for pre-digital times including neon colours and pastels, what broader home decor trends are doing. To me, social media is the place where folk art finds its home now. Within the vastness of these digital spaces, there are sub-communities and cultures that also spring up: folks who are part of the modern quilting movement often associated with the international Modern Quilt Guild, Tula Troops for fans of fabric designer Tula Pink, Canadian modern quilters, collectors of antique quilts, fashion designers that make clothing out of thrifted vintage quilts. Like hobbyists of all different types, it's possible—and quite easy—to find your people online. They don't have to live in your local community for you to connect, learn from, and geek out with. The product of these communities is reflective of culture, and not necessarily an individual's perspectives, putting it in the category (for lack of a better term) of folk art.

After many decades of toiling by many parties, the lines between folk art and fine art, craft and fine craft are starting to dissolve as the broader culture seeks to embrace expressions from more diverse sources. Traditional "women's work" can be a viable medium for artistic expression in the world of capital-A "art." And in that way, the collective nature of quilting can be seen as a positive quality, rather than one to be pooh-poohed.

QUILTS AS COLLECTIVE VOICE

Quilting represented an accessible way for women of diverse cultures and economic backgrounds to express voice, agency, and leave a mark by her own hand.

—Excerpt from the introductory text to *By Her Hand*, an exhibition of new works by Andrea Tsang Jackson and Marilyn Smulders, inspired by quilts in the Nova Scotia Museum collection.

A few years ago, I had the privilege of looking at a selection of quilts in the Nova Scotia Museum collection, alongside fellow quilt artist Marilyn Smulders. We set out to be inspired by them and create new works based on their patterns and stories. Assistant Curator Lisa Bower pulled out each quilt with care—some were in boxes, wrapped in archive-grade tissue, folded delicately; others were rolled onto poles and wrapped in clean old sheets and stored on racks in the archive. In my mind, one quilt in particular exemplifies the collective power of quilting.

Dated to early World War II, the red, white, and light blue quilt originated in Springhill, Nova Scotia, a coal mining town in the Cobequid Mountains. The quilt is made of two hundred squares on point— that is, oriented at forty-five degrees. The edge of the quilt is not trimmed to make a typical rectangular quilt; rather the points of each square diamond make a jagged but regular edge around the whole quilt. Within each square is a hand-embroidered name. Some were names of World War II soldiers, some were names of community members: "Margaret Akerley," "Leta Skidmore R.N.," "Curtis Williams," "Pte. K. L. Miller F78578." Toward the centre, one square is embroidered with a large V and its equivalent in Morse code; another says, "Hurrah! Canada!"

Each name represented a donation of twenty-five cents, enough for one war stamp. During the world wars, the Government of

Canada, like the United States, sold bonds, certificates, and savings stamps that helped fund the war effort. At the end of the war, the government would return the loaned funds with interest. All community members on the home front were encouraged to contribute what they could; even children were encouraged to save up their pennies, nickels, and dimes to buy stamps. A sheet of collected stamps represented a four-dollar bond, from which five dollars would be returned.

Like a donor wall that we might see in a major institution today, each square acknowledged monetary contributions—whether honouring a soldier or wartime nurse, or simply recognizing the name of the community member who donated funds. Across the squares, we could see that that many hands stitched these names. Some were more skillfully done, with even stitches and masterful navigation of the flourishes of cursive letters; other were shakier and more elementary. For women that couldn't make tangible contributions to the war effort through labour or military efforts, this was a way to raise their voices in support and exert agency in a time of war.

Signature quilts like this one were common ways for women to raise funds in their communities and speak into the public realm, and the concept was not limited to history or to wartime. In this same tradition, yet with a most contemporary interpretation, is Kim Soper's *In Our Own Words.* In March 2018, right around International Women's Day, Kim put out a call to quilters around the world to contribute 3½" × 6½" blocks, each with a word stitched in black on a white fabric

Andrea studying the war-time signature quilt from Springhill, Nova Scotia (Nova Scotia Museum, Cultural History collection, 2016.4). Photo credit: Marilyn Smulders.

background. The ask was a "…hand-stitched word of empowerment that describes YOU as a woman." She received blocks from thirty-one states and eight countries and the 196 words she received ranged from "intrepid" to "visible," "quirky," and "caring." My own contribution was "irrational," reclaiming a word historically used to degrade women and emotion. It is reflective of the way I think sometimes: instinctual and not reasoned. But I often come to the same truths as someone who might think about something in a step-by-step logical fashion.

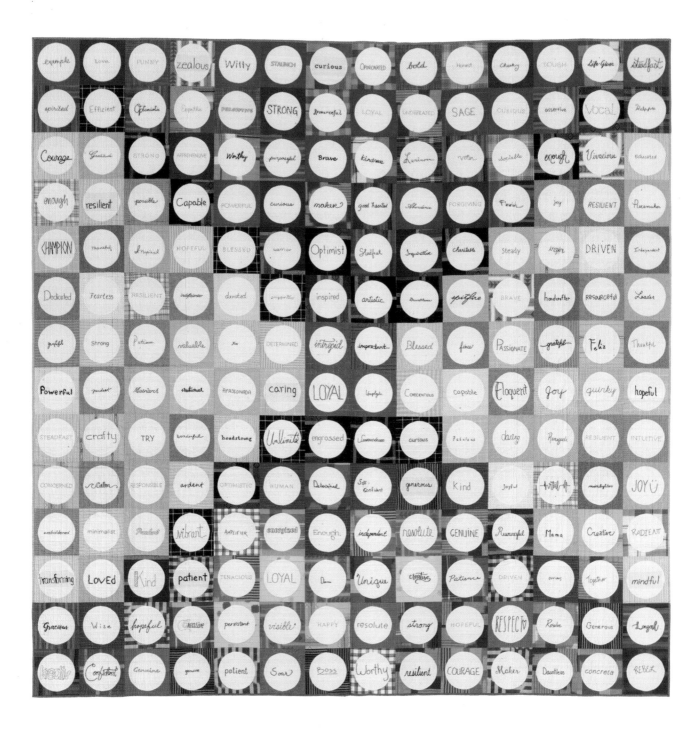

In Our Own Words
Kim Soper
2018
111 ½" × 111" (283 cm × 282 cm)
Quilted by Shelly Pagliai, Prairie Moon Quilts
Photo credit: International Quilt Museum,
University of Nebraska-Lincoln, 2021.039.0002.
Used with permission.

As Kim describes the project, "The words were...assembled into a quilt where each word was given equal significance. Each word was placed in its own circle, a nod to femininity and the cycles of nature; all of the fabrics used in the quilt are wovens, to represent our soft but unwavering strength; and the courthouse steps design, with the fire at the hearth center, is an homage to quilters past and present and collects all of the individual blocks into one, cohesive unit."

The quilt is massive—122 inches (248 centimetres) square—and is a mighty expression of the diversity of women's experiences and identifying descriptors. Women have much more agency in the economy and labour force in the twenty-first century than we used to have, so, unlike the signature quilt from Springhill, Nova Scotia, *In Our Own Words* is an explicit statement of powerful voices working together in community. *In Our Own Words* now resides at the International Quilt Museum in Lincoln, Nebraska, along with all the accompanying letters and notes Kim received from the participants who stitched their words.

QUILTS AS MONUMENTS

When we think of monuments, we think of spectacular statues and grandiose architecture in important cities. Epic promenades to awe-inspiring structures, and prior to the twentieth century, they memorialized deities, royalty, conquest, victory in battle—statements of religion, nationhood, and ruling powers. After the world wars, through its intersection with modernist architectural ideals, these types of commemorations fell out of favour. The architectural thinkers of the day spoke of democratization of places and spaces, including monuments. Something for the everyday man (definitely man and not woman), the little guy, for community life. Some such thinkers were Swiss nationals José Luis Sert, Fernand Léger, Siegfried Giedion. In their declaration entitled *Nine Points on Monumentality*, they begin by defining what monuments are:

- "...human landmarks which men have created as symbols for their ideals, for their aims, and for their actions.
- "...intended to outlive the period which originated them, and constitute a heritage for future generations, [forming] a link between the past and the future.
- "...an expression of man's highest cultural needs...the most vital are those which express the feeling and thinking of this collective force—the people."

How might a collective force be expressed through quilts? It doesn't seem like much of a stretch if you are a quilter. But thinking of quilts as monuments might seem a little more far-fetched.

In 1981, a new disease appeared in California, killing more than a hundred people during the first six months after its emergence. By 2012, a little over thirty years later, more than 600,000 Americans had died from AIDS. Then and now, people from all walks of life—family and friends, community members, actors, politicians, athletes—fight for research funding to treat this devastating disease and commit to awareness campaigns to help mitigate its spread and break the stigma around it. And no other campaign was as visible as the AIDS Memorial Quilt.

Conceived in 1985 by AIDS activist Cleve Jones, whose friends were dying from the disease, the AIDS Memorial Quilt sought to bring attention to the AIDS crisis. Jones made the first cloth panel marked with the name of his late friend Marvin Feldman. It measured three feet by six feet—roughly the size of a human grave. Eight of these panels were sewn together to make one block. Its inaugural showing in 1987 was on the National Mall in Washington, D.C. At the time, the quilt included 1,920 panels with 1,920 names, each one representing someone who had fallen to the disease, and made by victims' family members and friends. Its power propelled it on a twenty-city tour, raising hundreds of thousands of dollars for AIDS service organizations. And the quilt kept growing.

The AIDS Memorial Quilt is now an epic work, weighing fifty-four tons and dedicated to more than 110,000 individuals. Because of the medium, it can be packed up and moved to another city. With enough space, it can be displayed in its entirety, but it can also be broken up into sections without diluting its power. Since 2020, it has been digitized and is fully online and searchable. Through this monumental quilt, millions of dollars have been raised to support medical research and care, awareness and education. Today, the prognosis for those living with HIV/AIDS is significantly less dire than it was, and a quilt panel emblazoned with the phrase "THE LAST ONE," which was submitted to the project in 1987, will hopefully be a reality in the near future.

The AIDS Memorial Quilt is, in the words of those post-war Swiss architectural thinkers, a "symbol for people's ideals, aims, and actions." It "constitutes a heritage for future generations" and "links the past to the future." It "expresses the feeling and thinking of a collective force."

We make monuments when we make memory quilts out of a loved one's old clothes. We make monuments—a collective wish—when we make signature quilts to raise money for a war effort. We make monuments when we go through a deceased guildmate's fabric stash, distribute it, and make new things with it. We make monuments when we participate in community initiatives like raising money for our neighbourhood schools, local community organizations, make quilts for the Social Justice Sewing Academy (SJSA) Memorial Quilt Project[3] or Quilts for Survivors[4] or Quilts of Valour[5]. These quilts, although they seem minuscule compared to the size of the AIDS Memorial Quilt, are monuments that speak of shared loss or collective aspirations, and link us with hope to future generations.

---

3   sjsacademy.org/memorial-quilts. Memorial Quilts are textile memorials for families who have lost a loved one to violence, reflecting the life of the person in a quilt created using textiles or photos provided by their family.

4   quiltsforsurvivors.ca. Quilters from across Canada create quilts for survivors of the Residential School System and survivors of other trauma.

5   quiltsofvalour.ca. Quilts of Valour honour injured Canadian Armed Forces members past and present with quilts of comfort.

46th Annual Smithsonian Folklife Festival CREATIVITY AND CRISIS: UNFOLDING THE AIDS MEMORIAL QUILT Program on the National Mall in Washington, DC, on Wednesday afternoon, 4 July 2012. Photo credit: Elvert Barnes Photography. Creative Commons Attribution-ShareAlike 2.0 Generic license.

FAST AND FURIOUS, BUT ALSO BEAUTIFUL

Just a few years after the signature quilt was made in Springhill, Nova Scotia, a town built for 75,000 residents appeared in eastern Tennessee, seemingly overnight.

If you've watched the biopic *Oppenheimer* or read the book it's based on, *American Prometheus*, by Kai Bird and Martin J. Sherwin, you will understand the urgency and speed with which the U.S. military developed the science behind the atomic bomb. J. Robert Oppenheimer, a theoretical physicist and director of the Manhattan Project, was dubbed the "father of the atomic bomb." Key to the operation to develop the bomb was bringing the world's best scientific minds together to work furiously together with the mission to end Hitler's Nazi regime. The Manhattan Project was based in a purpose-built city in New Mexico named Los Alamos, where the scientists came to develop the mechanisms of the bomb. Simultaneously, two other sites, or "sister cities," were built to support the secretive project—Richland in Washington State, and Oak Ridge in Tennessee. A sign at the entrance of Oak Ridge read, "What You See Here, What You Do Here, What You Hear Here, When You Leave Here, **Let It Stay Here.**"

What was remarkable about the Oak Ridge community was its design. Charged with orchestrating the way these scientists and their families lived, architecture and engineering firm Skidmore, Owings & Merrill also had to create an attractive suburban community to get them to agree to move to this enclave in the first place. And they had to do it quickly. Military barracks—a logical, efficient, and economical solution—just would not do for these folks who had been called upon to leave their cushy lives. Among the dormitories, apartments, supermarkets, restaurants, school, and theatres, were modern and comfortable single-family homes surrounded by green spaces. It sounds like a regular suburb to most of us, but for the U.S. government to fund such a community and build it quickly was quite a feat. The key technology that made this possible was the pre-fabrication of modular homes.

Modularity allows for sections of buildings to be constructed off-site in production facilities, then transported to the site of their erection. Modules are often designed so they can be placed in various configurations—side-by-side, stacked, interlocking—like Lego bricks that click into place. These are based on two- and three-dimensional grids. The connections that attach the units together are well-considered parts of the design, keeping the elements out and maybe even having an aesthetic or decorative function.

Another modular architecture experiment-become-reality version of modular building is Montréal's Habitat 67, built for the World Expo and designed by then-graduate student Moshe Safdie. This series of apartments looks like bricks, arranged and stacked in various ways to make different indoor configurations, and their arrangements make diverse types of outdoor spaces. Uniform units built-off site, brought together to make a whole.

Traditional quilts are based on modules—block units sewn together with connections called sashing and cornerstones, which can be design elements in themselves. In the case of modern quilts, these connectors are often done away with completely. These block units, whether they are repetitive or unique like in a sampler, are easily assembled because they are the same dimensions. It makes collaborative efforts relatively straightforward. Each quilter makes a block of X or Y design in a harmonious colour palette, on their own "production" premises off-site (a.k.a. sewing room, studio, corner of the living room). They bring the blocks together in one place. Someone sews them together. Someone provides batting and backing. Someone quilts it. Someone prepares a label. Someone binds it. Yet another parallel to how craft guilds of earlier centuries worked—for craftspeople to specialize and offer a unique skillset to their group—is found in those collaborators: those who own a longarm quilting machine, those who love binding, those who have an embroidery machine to make labels, those who possess administrative abilities to organize group projects.

Inherently, quilts are modular, inviting the simplest and most efficient ways of making *together*. Collaboration is built into most quilt patterns. Some are more adventurous in the ways they collaborate. For example, the parameters of group quilts, also known as "bee" quilts, could be improvised blocks of varying sizes with a unifying palette and theme, allowing individual creativity within a set of rules. The AIDS Memorial Quilt is a similar take on a collaborative quilt.

Physical location used to be a determining factor in how bee quilts were made. In fact, quilting bees were gatherings of local community. With quilters connected across the world through social media, collaborative quilts are no longer location-dependent and reflect a cultural ethos that extends beyond geography, as in the case of *In Our Own Words* (see page 66). Bee quilts can be more intentional—you can be intentionally selective about who your bee includes to have a more specific vision that highlights individual expression in a collaborative context.

The image of multiple women gathered around a quilting frame is easily evoked when we say the word, "quilter." Collective power is inherent to the craft of quilting. When we look at it in light of craft guild history, folk art, monuments, collective voice, and modularity, we see how collective power shows up in different ways. We can lean on each other—for knowledge of our craft, for a specific bit of fabric that we are short of, to help our community at large through quilting. We can make wishes together and wrap our families, friends, and communities in them. ✕

Atlas of Quests

Although there has never been a documented account of a real-life treasure map leading to a priceless stash of loot, the idea of "X marks the spot" is widely understood in the popular imagination. The notion that there's a chest full of gold or jewels planted somewhere, just waiting to be uncovered by a chosen holder of the map, makes for a very captivating plot. In fact, it's the loose blueprint for many different types of stories: a lost child in search of family, an adventurer seeking purpose in life, a misfit that looks to belong somewhere. These are all stories of searching and exploring—of quests.

The word "quest" comes from the Latin word *quaerere*, which means "to seek" or "to question" (so it's no surprise that it also gave us the words "question" and "query"). In this section, we'll take some of the ideas described in the essays and apply them to explorations in quilting. For me, the conceptual ideas within the essays play out in—and intersect with— the practicalities of these quilt designs framed as quests.

This atlas is a collection of quests that I journeyed through in the process of making five quilts. Each quest sets us off on an expedition to find answers. Admittedly, the quests are self-serving. I had my own questions to ask and quilts that I wanted to make, so I serve as your tour guide even while embarking on my own process of thought and design, and I share some techniques along the way. Some of the quests contain a technical or creative exercise. In all but the last quest, you can bypass any of the exercises and just make the same quilt I made if desired. The last quest, however, is the most personal, so it will be unique to you. Each quest has a visual map of the paths you can follow, where you can stop off, and where you can end your journey.

In each quest, there is the option to start small and expand outward. Most do not have precise fabric requirements or explicit finished dimensions. They are for you to try something new and add to a library of techniques that you can call upon when needed.

It's best to approach the quests with an open mind—you might like a particular approach or technique, and you might not, but it's worth giving it a go. It's a way to develop the muscle of trying new things with only a small input—a bit of time and a bit of fabric. The outcome might be that you discover you absolutely love the process or one aspect of the technique, and you carry it forward. Another outcome might be that you really don't like it, and you can put it aside. Either possibility provides some insight into yourself.

The series of five quests is ordered in a specific way. *Trellis* and *Still Life* are relatively linear—one thing leads to another, which leads to the next. The next three quests—*House*, *Era*, and *Fogo II*—become increasingly open-ended, with design exercises that could lead you off into territory that is not explicitly mapped out. Even so, I try to give you something to lean on, such as a suggested layout or ways of thinking about how to design your own blocks. You are also welcome to blaze your own trail. And remember that sometimes the treasure remains elusive at the end of the story, and both the protagonist and reader come to accept that outcome.

ELEMENTS

Geographical features inform a journey—where you want to stop, what you want to avoid, how you will travel. Our elements are the traditional elements of art but applied specifically to quilting. The following glossary, in conjunction with the quilt *Mod Fire* pictured on page 74, is a visual legend to help us describe these elements and give us language to describe our quilts.

COLOUR

Gradient. A gradient is a series of colours that shift incrementally from one colour to the next. Sometimes the series includes just one hue (cream to beige [1]), and sometimes it includes more than one hue (pink to blue [2]).

Warm/Cool. The colour wheel is often divided in half, where the purest pinks, reds, oranges, and yellows are deemed warm colours while greens, blues, and purples are cool colours. However, most colours are not pure, and

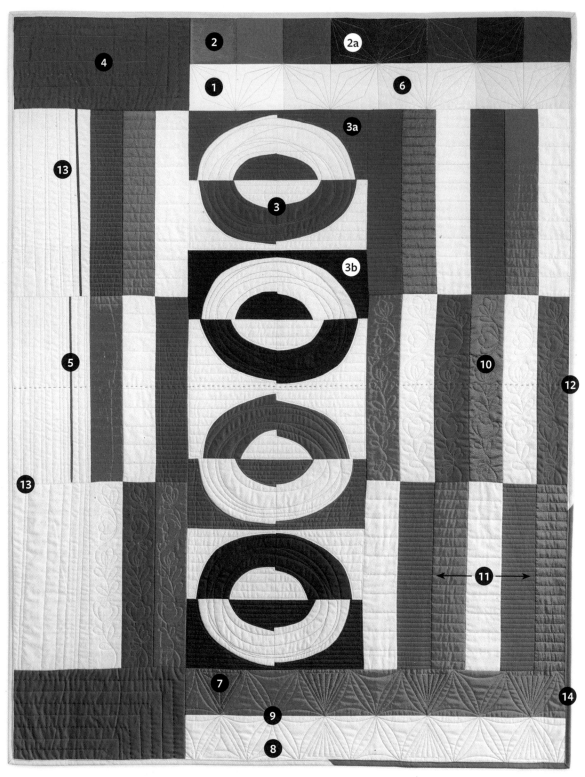

Mod Fire
50" × 64" (127 cm × 163 cm)
Quilted by Sheri Lund, Violet Quilts

usually have warm or cool undertones. For example, if a blue veers toward green, it is warmer (teal), and if it steers toward purple, it is cooler (perwinkle). If a purple has more red in it, it is warmer (plum [2a]), and if it has more blue in it, it is cooler (violet), as seen at the top of *Mod Fire*.

Neutrals have little to no colour [1]. Their hues are black, grey, and white. However, they can also be tinted and shaded colours; a very dark blue could be navy and neutral, or a very light yellow could be cream.

Saturation describes how pure a colour is. If it contains no black or white, it is saturated (e.g., red). If it is lightened with white (pink) or darkened with black (maroon), the colour is less saturated and becomes muted. Words that describe audio volume—loud, muted, dampened—are often used to characterize colour. There are two types of blue in *Mod Fire*, a saturated, pure blue [3a] and a darker, less saturated blue [3b].

LINE

A line is a moving dot. Lines can be formed in many different ways in quilting.

Stitches, whether by hand or by machine, create a line. Different kinds of thread create different kinds of lines [4].

Quilting, where layers are stitched together, is a series of lines.

Bias tape is a strip of fabric that is placed on top of another piece of fabric and stitched down, as in the *Trellis* quilt (page 78).

An inset strip is a strip of fabric that is pieced into another piece of fabric to make a line [5].

Text is a series of lines that offer a specific message through written language.

TEXTURE

Texture is the feel, appearance, or consistency of a surface or substance.

Print fabrics give the appearance of texture [6]. Solid fabrics can give a flatter appearance.

Quilting gives cloth texture because of the depth of the batting between the quilt's layers. Different types of batting (cotton, cotton/polyester, wool, bamboo) and quilting density create different types of texture.

Fabric types also have different kinds of texture. A cotton/linen blend is woven with a thicker warp and weft and will appear more textured than a quilting cotton, which is smoother because its warp and weft are finer. *Mod Fire* includes some Dupioni silk, which is shiny and textured and contains pink and black fibres, some of which are chunky [7].

Washing a fabric will give it more texture than an off-the-bolt piece of fabric that is treated during manufacturing.

SHAPE/FORM

Closed lines give rise to shapes and forms.

- Lines at 90 degrees give us squares and rectangles.
- Lines at 60 degrees give us equilateral triangles [7] [8], hexagons [9], and diamonds.

Polygons are closed shapes that have straight sides. Regular polygons have sides that are all the same length. Irregular polygons have sides that are different lengths.

Irregular shapes abound all around us, for example, in nature or when we draw freehand.

Repetition/rhythm. Repeating shapes give us rhythm. For example, a repeating pattern of stripes has a regular rhythm [10]. Repeating blocks provide modularity to the construction of the quilt.

Curves can be regular (such as circles and ovals) or irregular (such as crescents or blobs) [3].

Shapes and forms in quilting can be created by:

- Piecing fabrics together
- Appliqué, by applying fabric on top of a background, like a collage
- Reverse appliqué, by layering multiple fabrics and then taking away some of the top layer

DEPTH

Value is the relative lightness or darkness of a colour.

Scale is the relative size of something. A large-scale quilt block is one that is larger than "normal." Scale can also be used to describe the size of the motifs on print fabrics or the density of quilting [11].

Layering in quilting can refer to literal layers of fabric, as in appliqué or reverse appliqué, or making a quilt sandwich (quilt top, batting, and backing). It can also refer to the visual effect of shapes overlapping each other [7] [8] [9].

Symmetry is an exact mirror image along an axis. **Asymmetry** is a lack of symmetry. *Mod Fire* has an axis of symmetry marked by a heavy hand-quilted line [12]; however, it is not perfectly symmetrical in shape or colour—just *mostly* symmetrical.

Opaque, translucent, and transparent are words used to describe an effect of light. Transparent objects, like a clear window, allow light to pass through so objects on the other side can be clearly seen. Translucent objects, like a sheer curtain, let some light through, while opaque objects, like a wall, let no light through. Fabric can be opaque or translucent to different degrees (like silk or lace). Opaque quilting cottons can also give the illusion of transparency and translucency when the colours are well-chosen [7] [8] [9].

EDGE

Negative space is the empty space around the subject of an image [13]. Traditional quilts often have borders around a regular grid of blocks, as well as sashing in between the blocks, and cornerstones at the intersections of the sashing. These are all areas of negative space.

Binding is the most common way that a quilt is finished around the edges [14]. It is a narrow strip of fabric that covers the raw edges of the typical three layers of a quilt: quilt top, batting, and backing. It shows on both the front and back of a quilt.

Facing is an alternative way of finishing the edges of a quilt, where the finishing fabric strip is turned to the back of the quilt, so it does not show on the front.

IN BETWEEN

Contrast is the difference between two elements. Contrast can be high, as in a stark or noticeable difference between two elements, or low, as in a subtle difference between two elements.

Words used to describe the relationship between two or more elements:

- **Interplay** is the relationship between two or more elements that interact with each other (e.g., the interplay between the saturated pink and blue results in a high-contrast composition).

- **Adjacency** is the placement of two or more elements next to each other in a noteworthy way (e.g., the skinny blue stripe is adjacent to the large blue stripe that follows the regular rhythm of the strip sets, bringing attention to the slant of the skinny one.)

- **Tension** or **dissonance** occurs when elements don't quite make logical or visual sense together but contribute to the work by creating an energy between them.

- **Movement** is created when lines or another series of elements lead our eyes on a path around a piece. ⚉

Quest No. 1

Trellis

QUEST: Explore Line & Structure

Swiss artist Paul Klee is famously quoted as saying, "A line is a dot that went for a walk." A line can be straight or it can meander. It can be rigid or it can be free. A perfect vector line on the computer or a child's crayon scribble. A meticulously straight line with perfectly equal stitch lengths or a freeform hand-stitched line. A premeditated form or a stream of consciousness.

How can line be expressed in quilting?

QUEST MAP

Your journey through *Trellis* can meander, detour, or end where you want.

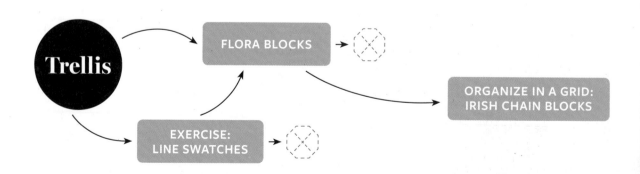

A selection of the drawings from my 100-Day Project, 2022.

A few years ago, I attempted a 100-Day Project. My goal was to draw something every day, using a brush pen on 4" × 6" index cards. It was a quick, small exercise to get me doing something creative on a regular basis. Each drawing would take me a minute or two, so some days I did two or three, and other days I managed ten, depending on if I had ideas. I repeated many motifs because I liked them, especially the botanical ones that I would try to recreate using a single stroke of the brush pen.

In *Building Containers* (page 30), I gave an overview of my fascination with translating a drawing from my notebook to fabric and the years-long exploration of line that started there. The 100-Day Project[1] and this fascination had nothing to do with one another—until a few months later, when I had a vision to create floral "drawings" with the fusible bias tape I had been using in my quilt work—and they suddenly had *everything* to do with each other. For me, these organic lines needed boundaries or a structure to organize them.

A trellis provides a structure on which something can grow. Vines punctuated with flowers and leaves grow upward, winding themselves up and around the frame. In the quilt *Trellis,* the traditional *Irish Chain* quilt pattern gives a sense of order to the wildness of the flowers.

Throughout the following exploration of line, we will use grids to help us structure our lines.

1   And for anyone who is wondering, I got to Day 74 of the challenge.

Exercise: Line Swatches

There are at least a hundred ways to make a line in quilting. In this exercise, we will focus on four: hand stitching, inset strip, machine double stitching, and bias-tape appliqué. From there, you can take your explorations as far and wide as you want by repeating and expanding the exercise.

After making some sample blocks using these four methods, we will make a more complex bias-tape appliqué block, testing the limits of the material. If you choose to make more of these blocks, like I did, you could organize them in combination with simple nine-patch blocks to form a traditional *Irish Chain*—our trellis.

MATERIALS

Fabric
- Fifteen 5" (12.5 cm) squares of background fabric (light colour, solid, blender, or low volume)
- One 8" (20 cm) square of black or other dark fabric (solid or blender)

Thread
- Two spools of 50 wt cotton or polyester thread in black or other dark colour (for use with a twin needle)
- Hand-sewing thread in black or other dark colour in at least two heavier weights, such as embroidery floss, 8 wt, 12 wt, or 30 wt—whatever you have on hand

Other Supplies
- ⅓ yd (0.3 m) Pellon® 950F ShirTailor® fusible interfacing, which comes in 20" (51 cm) width
- ½ yd (0.5 m) ¼"-wide fusible bias tape (like Clover Quick Bias) in black or another dark colour
- Quilting gloves
- 3-mm twin needle
- Hand-sewing needle
- Water-soluble fabric marker
- Fabric glue pen
- Seam ripper
- Rotary cutter and cutting mat
- Quilting ruler
- Iron
- Zipper foot

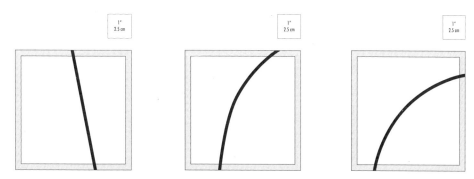

Photocopy these templates at 400% scale or download them at 3rdstoryworkshop.com/quilting-book#trellis. Grey indicates seam allowance.

Prepare the Squares

1. Following the manufacturer's instructions, fuse the Pellon® ShirTailor® interfacing onto the wrong side of six of the 5" (12.5 cm) squares.

2. Group the fifteen 5" (12.5 cm) squares into five sets of three; you will have three sets without interfacing and two sets with interfacing.

3. Using a water-soluble fabric marker, trace the three lines from the templates on page 81 onto each set of squares (one line per square).

Set 1: Hand Stitch

With the first set of non-interfaced squares, sew a running stitch along the marked lines using the lighter-weight hand-sewing thread. Knot the thread at the beginning and end of each stitch line. Remove the marked lines with water.

Set 2: Hand Stitch

Repeat the process from Set 1 with the second set of non-interfaced squares using your heavier-weight hand-sewing thread.

Set 3: Inset Strip

This technique is adapted and expanded, with permission, from Stephanie Ruyle's inset seaming tutorial on her blog (see the *Resources* section).

1. Cut the dark-coloured 8" (20 cm) square in half diagonally to form two triangles. From the triangles, sub-cut at least three strips along the bias measuring ¾" (2 cm) wide. See Figure 1.

2. Using the remaining set of non-interfaced background squares, start with the square marked with the straight line. Fold the fabric along the marked line, right sides together, and press. Using the longest stitch available on your machine and a **generous** (not scant) ¼" (6 mm) seam allowance, baste a line along the folded edge. Using the rotary cutter and quilting ruler, trim off the folded edge, removing as little fabric as possible. Press the seam open. See Figure 2.

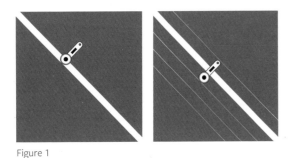

Figure 1

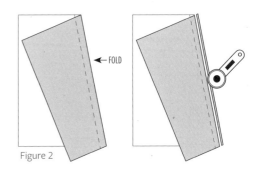

← FOLD

Figure 2

3. With the wrong side of the square facing up, apply a thin line of glue onto the opened part of the seam allowance. Try to keep the glue away from the centre basted seam.

4. Centre one ¾" (2 cm) strip of inset fabric on top of the glued seam, right side down. Press the unit from both sides to set the strip in place. See Figure 3.

5. Install the zipper foot on your machine and reset your stitch length to normal.

6. Turn the unit over so the right side is up (Figure 4a). Flip the background fabric on the right side onto the fabric on the left

side, right sides together, exposing the basted seam. Using your zipper foot, sew a parallel line just to the right of the basted seam (Figure 4b). You will be sewing through one layer of the inset fabric and one layer of the background fabric. The distance between the basted seam and this stitch line is *about half the width of your inset*. No need to be precise with this measurement for these blocks; we're just aiming for "skinny."

7. Repeat Step 6 to sew a line next to the basted seam on the left side of the unit (Figure 4c).

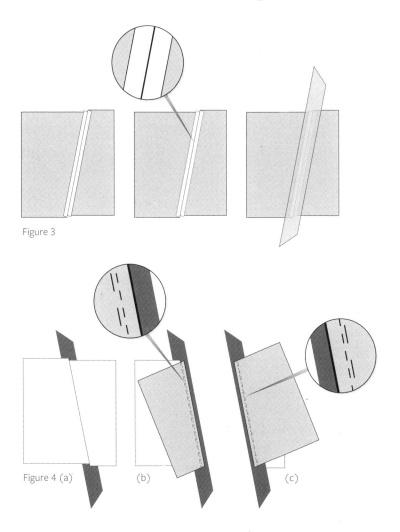

Figure 3

Figure 4 (a)   (b)   (c)

8. Place your block right side up. Use your seam ripper to carefully remove the basting stitches (Figure 5a).

9. Pull the seam and glue apart and press open with some steam (Figure 5b). If there is glue left in the seam, it can be washed out. *Note:* The width of the line may not be uniform along its length, which is one of the great features of this technique.

10. Trim the top and bottom of the block to a straight edge, removing the excess length from the inset strip (Figure 5c). *Note:* Unlike all our other exploration blocks, these blocks will not end up being 5" (12.5 cm) square.

11. Repeat this process using the other two squares in the set (marked with the gently curved line and the curve that is more like a quarter-circle) (Figure 6). For Step 2, finger press the curve before pressing with the iron. Because the ¾" (2 cm) strips are cut on the bias, they will bend easily to accommodate the curve. (This is a technique that I adapted from UK quilter Jenny Haynes's teachings; she is an expert at sewing skinny inset curves. See the *Resources* section.) For Step 10, trim all four sides of these blocks to a straight edge.

Set 4: Double-Stitch Line

Install the 3-mm twin needle in your machine. Then, load the machine with the two spools of 50 wt black thread, keeping the two threads parallel as they are threaded through the needle.

With the first set of interfaced squares, sew along the marked lines using your double stitch, centring the marked line between the two needles. Backstitch at the start and end of each stitch line. Remove the marked lines with water.

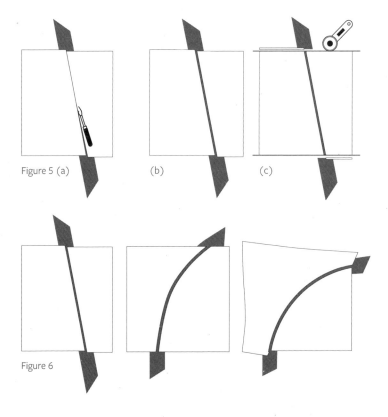

Figure 5 (a) (b) (c)

Figure 6

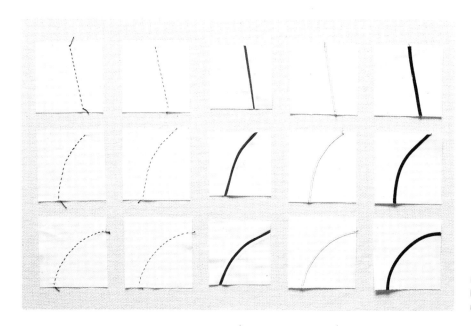

Below: A series of expanded line blocks, with some added negative space.

Set 5: Fusible Bias Tape

On the remaining set of interfaced squares, fuse a strip of bias tape on top of each of the marked lines. Trim the ends of each strip, aligning the cut-line with the edge of the square. Stitch along each strip of bias tape with a double stitch to secure it in place, backstitching at the start and end.

Sew the Swatches Together

Experiment with more blocks if you wish (see *Expand* on page 86 for some ideas).

Arrange your swatches in a grid. You will need to add some fabric to the width and/or length of the inset-strip swatches to make them 5" (12.5 cm) square.

Sew the squares, right sides together, into rows using a scant ¼" (6 mm) seam allowance, then sew the rows together.

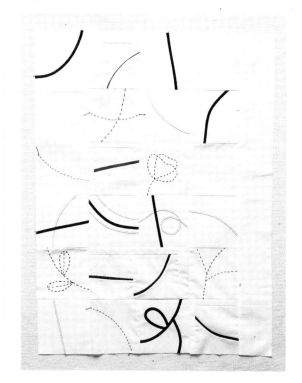

For the double stitch and fusible bias tape techniques, wear quilting gloves to help manoeuvre the fabric.

- Vary the stitch length and/or spacing of your hand stitches.
- Try different hand stitches, such as a back stitch, stem stitch, or chain stitch.
- Knot your thread on top of the fabric, rather than on the back.
- Have the ends of the line start and stop on adjacent edges or the same edge of the square.
- Test the limit of the curvature of a line with your double stitch or fusible bias tape. How tight can the curve be?

- Add multiple lines on each square.
- Intersect lines.
- Turn some of the blocks when arranging them to vary their orientation.
- Make a loop-de-loop.
- Think about how the lines will interact with quilting lines that might be sewn later.
- Combine different techniques within the same square.

Flora Blocks

Now that you are getting comfortable using fusible bias tape, we will try a slightly more complicated block using a floral motif.

MATERIALS

- One 9½" (24 cm) square of background fabric (light colour, solid, blender, or low volume) per block
- 2 spools of 50 wt cotton or polyester thread in black or other dark colour (for use with a twin needle)
- One 9½" (24 cm) square of Pellon® 950F ShirTailor® fusible interfacing per block
- One roll of ¼"-wide fusible bias tape (like Clover Quick Bias) in black or other dark colour (one 11-yd roll will make approximately 7 *Flora* blocks)
- Quilting gloves
- 3-mm twin needle
- Water-soluble fabric marker
- Iron

Prepare the Squares

- Following the manufacturer's instructions, fuse the Pellon® ShirTailor® interfacing onto the wrong side of the background fabric.
- Choose one of the *Flora* templates from page 87. Align the edges of the *Flora* template with the edges of the fabric, as indicated. Using a water-soluble fabric marker, trace the lines onto the fabric.

Fuse the Bias Tape

1. Pull a length of fusible bias tape a bit longer than the line marked #1 on the template. Do not cut the bias tape.
2. Lay the start of the tape on top of the marked line on your fabric. Trim the start of the tape to match the approximate angle at the start of the line. See Figure 7.

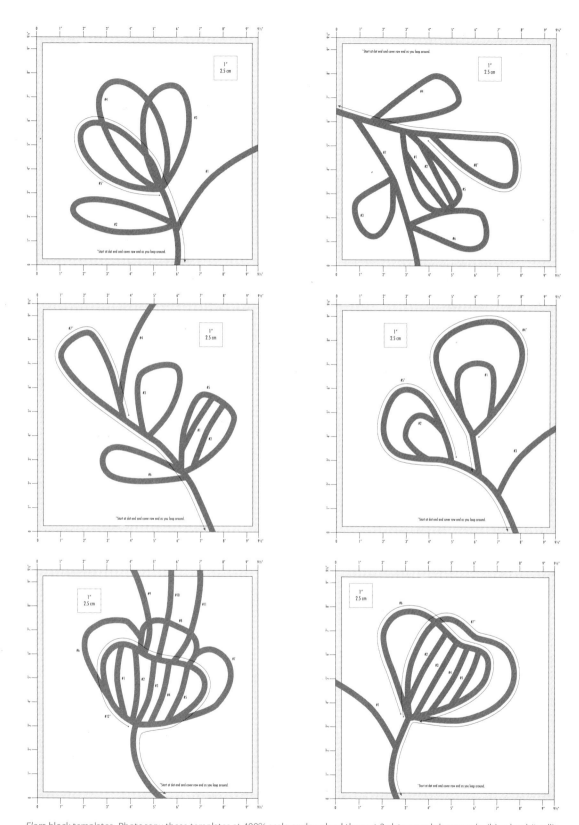

Flora block templates. Photocopy these templates at 400% scale or download them at 3rdstoryworkshop.com/quilting-book#trellis. Grey indicates seam allowance.

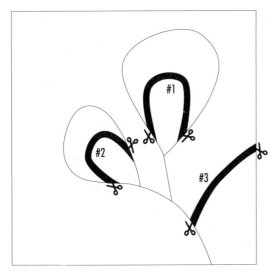

Figure 7

5. Trim the tape to match the approximate angle where the line ends and press once more to fully fuse.

6. Sew down the bias tape using a twin needle and two spools of thread. Backstitch at the start and end of the line.

7. Repeat Steps 1–6 with the subsequent lines on the template, working in numerical order. You can fuse multiple strips at a time as long as they don't intersect. Be sure to sew down each strip before layering any intersecting strips on top. When adding intersecting strips, cover the raw edges of the previous strip with the new strip.

3. Peel the paper backing from the bias tape for roughly the length of the entire line. Gently lay the tape down along the marked line, aligning the centre of the tape with the line as best you can.

4. Use your iron to fuse the tape down. For longer lengths, you can peel back the paper and lay out the tape bit by bit in smaller sections.

Note: The "start" of the line can be at either end. If you are right-handed, it might feel more natural to go from right to left, with your iron in your right hand. If you are left-handed, it might feel more natural to go from left to right, with your iron in your left hand.

Make as many *Flora* blocks as you like.

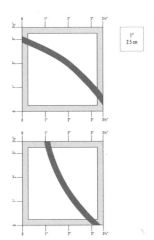
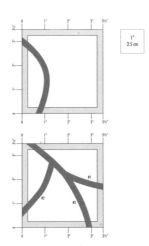
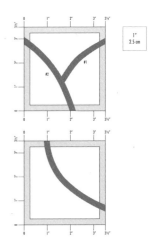

Stem Connector templates. Photocopy these templates at 400% scale or download them at 3rdstoryworkshop.com/quilting-book#trellis. Grey indicates seam allowance.

Organize in a Grid: *Irish Chain* Blocks

Note: Use fabric with a minimum 42" (107 cm) width of fabric (WOF).

MATERIALS

- One 1½" (4 cm) × WOF strip of black or other dark fabric; sub-cut as follows:
  - A: Two 1½" × 16" (4 cm × 40.5 cm)
  - B: One 1½" × 8" (4 cm × 20 cm)

- From white or other light fabric, cut
  - One 1½" (4 cm) × WOF strip; sub-cut as follows:
    - A: One 1½" × 16" (4 cm × 40.5 cm)
    - B: Two 1½" × 8" (4 cm × 20 cm)
  - Four 3½" (9 cm) squares

1. Using a scant ¼" (6 mm) seam allowance,[2] sew the dark A strips to the top and bottom of the light A strip. Press toward the dark strips. See Figure 8a.

2. Using a scant ¼" (6 mm) seam allowance, sew the light B strips to the top and bottom of the dark B strip. Press toward the dark strip. See Figure 8b.

3. Sub-cut the A strip set into ten 1½" (4 cm)-wide units. Sub-cut the B strip set into five 1½" (4 cm)-wide units.

4. Group two A units and one B unit into a nine-patch block as shown (Figure 8c). Sew the units together using a scant ¼" (6 mm) seam allowance, then press the seam allowance open. Repeat to make a total of 5 nine-patch blocks.

Optional: If you would like to add stem connectors to any of the four 3½" (9 cm) light squares, use any of the templates on page 88 and the method from Steps 1–7 of *Flora Blocks* above to add fusible bias tape. Interface the squares before adding the bias tape.

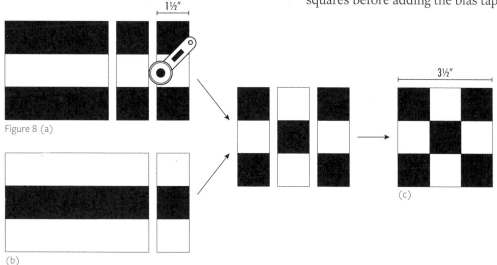

Figure 8 (a)

(b)

(c)

---

2 A scant ¼" seam allowance is a seam allowance that is slightly narrower than ¼" inch. It compensates for the loss of some fabric in the folds of a seam, so that the dimensions of your block remain true once they are pressed. Find out more at 3rdstoryworkshop.com/tutorial-what-is-a-scant-1-4.

5. Alternate the nine-patch blocks with the 3½" (9 cm) squares as shown (Figure 9). Sew the units, right sides together, into rows using a scant ¼" (6 mm) seam allowance, then sew the rows together to make 1 *Irish Chain* block. Press the seam allowances open or away from the nine-patch blocks.

Make as many *Irish Chain* blocks as you like.

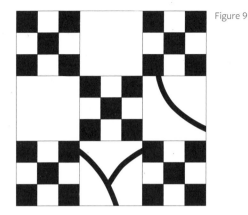

Figure 9

Optional: Make a Quilt

The table below lists the number of *Flora* and *Irish Chain* blocks you'll need for different sizes of the *Trellis* quilt. Remember that one 11-yard roll of bias tape will make approximately 7 blocks. You can use the web-based app PreQuilt to digitally mockup your own layout: 3rdstoryworkshop.com/quilting-book#trellis.

27" × 27" (69 cm × 69 cm)	45" × 45" (114 cm × 114 cm)
5 *Flora* blocks	13 *Flora* blocks
4 *Irish Chain* blocks	12 *Irish Chain* blocks

63" × 63" (160 cm × 160 cm)	81" × 81" (206 cm × 206 cm), as in sample
25 *Flora* blocks	41 *Flora* blocks
24 *Irish Chain* blocks	40 *Irish Chain* blocks

5 *Flora* blocks with 4 in-progress *Irish Chain* blocks.

ELEMENTS OF *TRELLIS*

Line. In this quest, we have tried a range of ways to make a line. They have different weights and qualities: thin, thick, broken, straight, heavy, wobbly. *Trellis* leans into the use of fusible bias tape, which yields a consistent and heavy line quality.

Neutral and Contrast. Fusible bias tape is readily available in only limited colours, the most common being black. *Trellis* was conceived as I drew continuous line sketches using a thick brush pen on index cards. Luckily, the black bias tape was a great mimic. This neutral, high-contrast, two-colour palette is a result of the parameters I placed on the design. Feel free to expand your fabric choices to suit what you have or simply what you like.

Symmetry/Asymmetry. This design is very symmetrical in some ways and very much not in other ways. The quilt is square, with *Flora* and *Irish Chain* blocks alternating in a regular rhythm. However, while the placement of the *Flora* blocks repeats in a symmetrical pattern, the floral motifs twist and turn in different ways within the blocks.

90 Degrees vs. Organic Lines. The most dynamic quality of the composition is the contrast of the square nine-patch blocks against the curving lines of the bias-tape florals. The quilting follows the same logic but reverses the placement: The straight lines frame the bias-tape blocks, and floral motifs overlay the nine-patch blocks. ✕

Trellis
81" × 81" (206 cm × 206 cm)
Quilted by Sheri Lund, Violet Quilts

Quest No. 2
Still Life

QUEST: Approach Quilting Like Painting

> What parallels can be drawn between painting and quilting? More specifically, what is underpainting, and how can it be translated to fabric?

Contemporary artist Helen Wells uses leftover paints on a palette to create abstract underpaintings in her sketchbook.[1] She then blocks out shapes by painting white or neutral paint on top. Berlin-based artist Katie Straus[2] works many of her paintings in a similar way, layering white paint over vibrant abstract shapes to create images of flowers in vessels. In quilting, I wondered what this type of reversal of figure (object) and ground (background) could create.

Opposite:
Still Life
30" × 40"
(76 cm × 102 cm),
mounted on canvas
Quilted by
Gillian Noonan

---

1   https://helenwellsartist.com/blogsandvideos/paintedpages
2   Katie Straus, katiestraus.com / Instagram: @katiestraus_art

QUEST MAP
Your journey through *Still Life* can meander, detour, or end where you want.

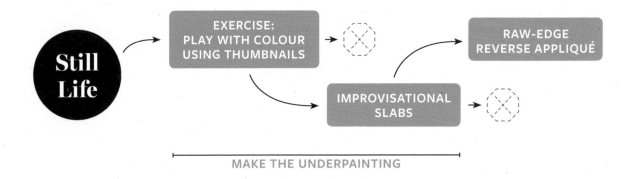

Underpainting & Surrender

Still Life has been an exercise in surrender for me. I had never made this type of quilt before, nor had I ever worked with such organic shapes. I even had to draft the instructions before the experiment was complete. I knew that I wanted the shapes to be reminiscent of a still life composition with flowers and vessels, like Katie Straus's paintings, so I started drawing vases over and over again. None of them seemed quite right, and I was not excited to move them to fabric.

It was not until I picked up some scrap bristol board and started cutting into it with scissors as my "drawing implement" that satisfactory shapes appeared. It was this act of simulating what was going to happen in fabric—large cutouts—where it started to make sense.

In the late 1940s, Henri Matisse worked with cutouts in the last period of his career, collaging brightly coloured papers together—first on a small scale and eventually at the scale of murals and rooms. He used scissors as his drawing implement, and this is the same approach I carried with me into my iteration of *Still Life*. And it worked. This pre-mimicking, where I "sketched" with scissors to imitate the way I would later be cutting into the fabric, was just the method I needed to get the right kind of shapes.

The technique of raw-edge reverse appliqué using jersey is not new. It is fashion house Alabama Chanin's signature technique, and fabric and quilt designer Alison Glass uses

In my thumbnail for *Still Life*, I chose only one fabric to represent each of the six hues with a pop or two of contrasting colours for each. When sewing my slabs later, I expanded the selection of fabrics within each hue.

this same method in the *Fountain* project from her book *Alison Glass Appliqué: The Essential Guide to Modern Appliqué*. Where *Still Life* departs from these other applications is its focus on the *underpainting*—the image that is being revealed as you remove the top layer of fabric. The underpainting is composed of *slabs*, or quilt blocks that are improvised using scraps. The concept and term comes from Cheryl Arkison and Amanda Jean Nyberg's book *Sunday Morning Quilts*, in which they describe how to sew scraps together to make a piece of fabric, usually in a single hue. In this quest, I want to invite you to construct a patchwork layer for the underpainting in a way that is intuitive rather than planned and to encourage you to make your own cutout shapes instead of using my templates if you so choose.

When I made my patchwork layer, I turned to a drawer I have that contains a mess of what I call "precious scraps." They are nonsensical sizes of fabrics that I really like—triangle offcuts, strips of varying widths, single bits of favourite florals—nothing useful for any one project. I dumped the drawer out onto my table and started sorting the scraps by colour. There were smaller bits of brightly coloured fabrics—poppy red, leftover oranges, small strips of a printed shimmery gold, a curry-like yellow—and a colour palette emerged that I was really drawn to. This makes logical sense, since they were my favourite fabrics, but I didn't imagine they'd make any sense together. I cut imprecise snippets of the fabrics and glued them to an index card. I had my favourite gold thread in my machine, so I sewed everything down with some simple straight lines. This thumbnail was my first "container" to experiment with colour adjacencies. We'll begin our *Still Life* exercise by making thumbnails to guide our colour choices for the underpainting slabs.

MATERIALS

For the thumbnail(s):
- Blank index cards (4" × 6" [10 cm × 15 cm]) or scraps of paper with the same dimensions
- Fabric scraps
- Glue stick
- Thread in complementary colour(s)

For the quilt:
- Same fabric scraps as above
- Paper scissors
- Bristol board or card stock
- 100% cotton jersey in white or your preferred colour, at least 2" (5 cm) wider and longer than your desired finished size or canvas size
- Quilting cotton for the backing fabric, at least 4" (10 cm) wider and longer than your desired finished size or canvas size. *Note:* If you plan to bind the quilt rather than mount it, this backing fabric will become the binding for the quilt. If you mount the quilt, this fabric will not be seen.
- No. 8 perle cotton in colour(s) that complement your fabric
- Water-soluble fabric marker
- Sashiko or hand-quilting needle
- Small, sharp fabric scissors
- *Optional:* Artist canvas, 30" × 40" (76 cm × 102 cm) (or desired finished size)

Exercise: Play With Colour Using Thumbnails

1. Dump a pile of scraps onto a table.
2. Press each piece of fabric and sort them by their dominant hue; in other words, by colour name—blues, reds, pinks, greens, etc. Be sure to lay them out so you can see each piece of fabric. You can overlap them, but do not stack them.
3. Observe:
   - **Proportions.** Is there a lot of one colour?
   - **Warm/Cool.** Do you tend toward pinks/reds/oranges/yellows or greens/blues/purples? Looking closer, are your hues warm or cool? For example, blues can veer warm (toward green) or cool (toward purple). Group them accordingly.
   - **Solids/Prints.** Do you have more prints or solids?
4. Decide what you want your underpainting to look like. Keep in mind that the overlay will be a bright white if you're following the sample.
   - **Monochromatic.** Do you want to focus on just one hue (for example, all your blues mixed together)?
   - **Analogous.** Do you want to use a few hues that sit adjacent on the colour wheel, like purple/red/pink?
   - **Sections of different hues.** This is the type of thumbnail that I used for the basis for the sample quilt. Edit down the number of hues to a maximum of six; this pre-selection will help you make decisions later.

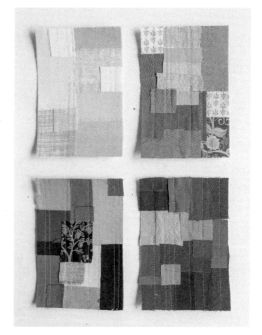

Four thumbnails: tinted neutral, monochromatic green, blues with pops of orange-red, and analogous. Each composition contains nine or fewer fabrics, although some fabrics are repeated.

   - **Muted or saturated.** I used muted colours—light, cool blue; dark navy; off-white; warm, earthy green; blush; rust—with bright, punchy accents.
   - **Pops of contrast.** For example, you could add little bits of white amongst a mix of blues.

5. Use your selected fabrics to make one or more thumbnails. (Build a container.)
   - Use an index card or scrap of paper as your base.
   - Pick five to nine fabrics to represent each hue group you will use to make a slab. Cut a small swatch of each fabric.
   - Arrange the swatches on an index card or scrap of paper.

- Pay attention to the proportions of colour you are laying down. If you decided on pops of contrast, add smaller swatches for those.
- Don't be too careful about the process. Simply ask: Do I like this? If the answer is yes, then proceed. If the answer is no, then rearrange or recut swatches, or start again.
- Once you're satisfied with the arrangement, glue the swatches down to the index card. They can overlap, and smaller swatches can be glued on top of larger swatches.
- Using your machine, sew the swatches down to the paper using a complementary thread colour.
- Repeat this process as many times as you like. Set a timer and see if you can make a composition in ten minutes or less.
- Choose one thumbnail to be the basis of your underpainting.

Make the Underpainting

1. **Make slabs.** Take one hue grouping and sew the scraps together in an improvisational manner.
   - Start by sewing two similarly sized scraps right sides together with a ¼" (6 mm) seam allowance. Press the seam open and trim any overhanging bits. See Figure 1.
   - Find a third scrap that is roughly the same length as the unit made from the first pair and sew it on. Press the seam open. See Figure 2.

- Continue to grow the fabric unit in this way. Create multiple pieces from the grouping using scraps that fit well together in terms of size and colour. Don't overthink how they go together, how big the units get, or what their overall shape is—add strips side by side, create triangular shapes, add new scraps perpendicular to the ones you've already sewn—anything goes, as in Figure 4.

Tip 1: If you are using pops of contrast, prepare smaller strips or rectangles of the contrasting fabric beforehand and incorporate them into some of the units.

Tip 2: Depending on how big your scraps are, you may end up creating a lot of intricate pieces or simpler ones with just a few seams in each. If the patchwork is chunkier than you'd like (as in the pieces of fabric seem too large to you), cut the unit into two uneven parts and sew them back together in a new arrangement, as in Figure 3.

Tip 3: Pressing your seams open will do you a favour when you're hand quilting later.

- Once you've made several pieces from the grouping, begin to lay them out in a square or rectangular arrangement (see Figure 4). Add on additional scraps as needed so the pieces will fit together, then sew these units together in the same improvisational manner and trim the edges to finish the slab. See Figure 5.

Figure 1

Figure 2

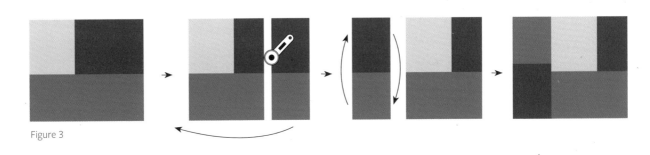

Figure 3

Figure 4

Figure 5

Tip 4: When you are coming to the edge of a slab, consider what fabrics will be in the adjacent slab according to your thumbnail. Add a strip to the edge of the slab that incorporates the colours of your current slab with the colours of the next one to help them transition.

◎ Repeat this process to create additional slabs for each part of your thumbnail. These could be in a similar hue but a different tone if you are aiming for a monochromatic composition or, like mine, be different hues altogether. For a finished quilt that is 30" × 40" (76 cm × 102 cm), aim to make six slabs that are approximately 17" × 15" (43 cm × 38 cm).

2. **Assemble the quilt.** Once the slabs are made, lay them out using your thumbnail as a guide. They probably won't be the right shapes and sizes to fit together. Add on additional scraps as needed or plan to trim off excess fabric after they're sewn together. Once you're happy with how the slabs align with each other, sew them together, them trim off any excess fabric so the composition is 2" (5 cm) wider and longer than your desired finished size or canvas size.

The assembled underpainting is a work in itself, and you could stop here and make a quilt from what you have created if you like.

From thumbnail to slab composition: In my thumbnail for *Still Life*, I chose only one fabric to represent each of the six hues with a pop or two of contrasting colours for each. When sewing my slabs later, I expanded the selection of fabrics within each hue.

Create the Cutouts

Let go. There will be bits of colour and adjacencies that you will love in your improvised slabs. The reality of reverse appliqué is that parts of your underpainting will be layered over. Before you proceed, you will need to surrender the idea of having total control over how these favourite parts will or will not show.

Compose. Photocopy the templates on page 102 at 400% scale or download them at 3rdstoryworkshop.com/quilting-book#still-life. You will also need a second copy of template P1 photocopied at 500% or the downloaded version printed at 125%. This will give you two pots of different sizes. If you are not following the sample layout, you can adjust the size of any of these shapes as desired.

Cut out each template along the inside solid line, then trace them onto bristol board or card stock. Cut the inside shape out, leaving a window or frame of the shape. Label each with the code on the template (P = pot, L = leaf, S = stem, and F = flower). Make multiples as you like. Arrange the shapes on top of your slab composition. You can lay them out like I have in my final piece or play around with the composition and number of shapes. You could do a single potted plant instead of two. You could make your own leaf, flower, and vase shapes. You could even use letter forms, like the Q on the cover of this book. You can also add additional shapes; in my sample, I added a top and bottom border to ground the composition, as shown in the layout diagram. Some shapes may need to overlap to create a single cutout in the final piece (like connecting the leaves to the

Template cutouts on "underpainting."

stem), but you need to leave at least ½" (1.5 cm) of space between unconnected shapes (where the jersey won't be cut away).

Record your results. Once you are happy with the composition, take a photo of it. Roughly measure the width and length of your layout so you can replicate it.

Cut your jersey and backing. For the top layer of your quilt, cut the jersey to the same size as your slab composition. For the backing, cut the quilting cotton 4" (10 cm) wider and longer than your composition.

Baste. To make a quilt sandwich, lay out the backing piece right side down and smooth it out. Tape it down to your surface to keep it taut. Centre the patchwork layer on top with a 2" (5 cm) border all the way around, followed by the top layer of jersey so that it is even with the patchwork layer. Baste with safety pins or by hand with a long basting stitch.

Prepare the overlay. Using your reference or the layout diagram, lay out your composition of shapes on top of the jersey. Using a water-soluble fabric pen, trace the shapes onto the jersey. Overlapped shapes should be traced as a single shape. Remove the templates. *Note:* You will not be able to place all the shapes exactly as in your reference photo, since the jersey overlay prevents you from seeing your colour composition fully. This is where we surrender. If you are not happy with the way the composition looks, remove some of the markings with a damp cloth and try again until you are satisfied. Do not cut anything out yet!

Raw-edge reverse appliqué. Using perle cotton and a sashiko or hand-quilting needle, stitch a running stitch around the *outside* of the traced shapes, about ⅛" (3 mm) to ¼" (6 mm) away from the drawn lines. When tying off a piece of thread, be sure to bury your knot between the backing and the patchwork layer.

After you have stitched around all the shapes, cut away the inner shapes, including the drawn lines, with small, sharp fabric scissors. Cut only through the jersey layer; be careful not to cut into your colour slabs! The wonderful thing about jersey is that it does not fray, so you can leave these edges unfinished.

Sample layout. If you are following the sample shown in the book, use this diagram to help you map out your composition. The outer dimensions are 30" × 40" (76 cm × 102 cm).

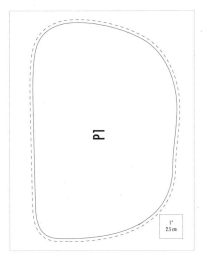

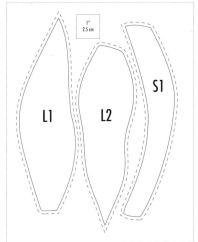

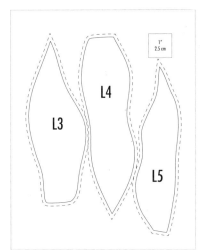

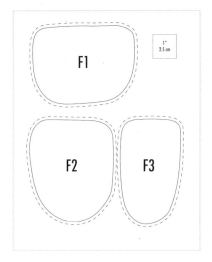

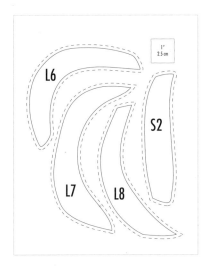

Still Life templates. Photocopy these templates at 400% scale or download them at 3rdstoryworkshop.com/quilting-book#still-life. Dotted line indicates roughly where the stitched line of the reverse appliqué will be.

Finishing

I mounted my *Still Life* onto canvas purchased from the art store. To edge the piece, I used a striped fabric to create facing strips, which I backed with interfacing to strengthen them. Quilt artist Kelly Spell offers a very helpful guide on her blog for mounting a quilt onto a framed canvas (see the *Resources* section).

Alternatively, if you'd like to finish your piece as a quilt, once the appliqué is complete, trim the patchwork and jersey layers to the same size. Be careful to not cut into the backing layer! Trim the backing to be 1" (2.5 cm) larger than the top two layers all the way around. Fold the excess backing onto itself, wrong sides together, so the edge of the backing meets the edge of the top layers. Then fold the backing edge again so it covers the edge of the top layers, creating a binding. Clip in place around the perimeter. Secure the binding using a top stitch on your machine or by hand sewing a running stitch with perle cotton along the edge of the binding through all three layers of the quilt.

Any point along this road could have been the destination. I found myself quite enamoured with my index-card thumbnails and would have been satisfied to stop there with this colour study. The thumbnail exercise could be an end in itself. I also really liked my slab colour composition, and that could have become a quilt on its own with no jersey overlay. I also loved the way the quilted piece looked before it was mounted. Taking each subsequent step was a leap of faith, a surrender to what could be next.

ELEMENTS OF *STILL LIFE*

Colour. The improvised slabs create adjacencies of warm and cool, saturated and muted, with the neutral white veiling a cacophony of colours.

Line. The contours of the quilting lines echo the contours of the shapes.

Texture. Stitch lines add subtle ripples to the surface and underpainting fabric.

Shape. Raw-edge appliqué lends itself well to rounded and contoured shapes.

Depth. The more saturated colours contrast with the white jersey. The literal layering of materials gives the piece depth, like you're looking through a window.

Edge. Broad swaths of negative space allow the colours to sing and breathe. The striped edge of the canvas gives the work a boundary and provides the viewer with a place to start and stop looking. ⏳

Quest No. 3

House

QUEST: Lead the Effort to Make a Group Quilt

How do you design a group quilt that appeals to people with different skill levels and interests?

QUEST MAP

Your journey through *House* can meander, detour, or end where you want.

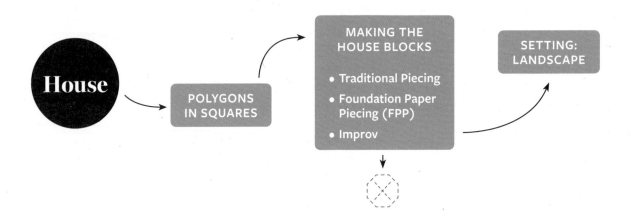

Form & Community

This book begins with the idea of having a safe place to return to. The notion of home is a recurring theme in my work and life; it is a place, both physical and emotional, that I operate from in all facets of my life and then return to when all is said and done.

Although I appreciate good house design and can endlessly consume photos and videos of immaculate and expansive homes on social media, I am not one to obsess greatly about having a perfectly designed space for me and my family. It's not that I don't want it; it's that my resources—time, finances, energy—are spoken for with other things that are more important to me at the moment.

What constitutes home for me is different from the walls and the roof, the artwork that hangs, or the colour of the hardwood. It's a good meal, it's people to laugh with, or it's a space for vulnerability.

If I asked you to draw a house, I think you'd conjure up something that looks like a square with a door, windows, and a peaked roof. Children from all over the world, when asked to draw a home or house, often draw the same thing. Very few of us live in a house that looks like this, but this five-sided form is a near-universal symbol of a vernacular house. It means something to everybody.

I made the first iteration of this quilt a few years ago for a friend and her family. She, like me, has a strong sense of home; it's the centre of her world. She has a family of five, and it seemed fitting that a five-sided shape could be the central shape of a quilt for them.

In *Corner Brook*, I used five different foundation paper piecing (FPP) templates, repeated throughout the design. FPP is a great technique for shapes that are not based on simple angles like 90°, 60°, 45°, or 30°. The outline of the block design is printed onto a paper template, and the fabric is sewn onto the paper using the lines as a guide. The paper is removed after the blocks are sewn together. Using the different FPP templates in *Corner Brook* gave the roof angles enough variety to look a bit random. For this reason, I also included an option in *House* for a few FPP blocks. While the exercise does not include instructions for the FPP technique, there are many online tutorials, which you can find in the *Resources* section.

House is the group rendition of *Corner Brook*. This project capitalizes on the modularity of quilt making, an idea that we explored in *Collective Power* (page 60). Each "house" unit in the quilt has the same dimensions, but can appeal to different preferences and skills. *House* provides traditional piecing, FPP, and improv versions of the block. Each technique can also be a simple introduction for someone who wants to learn a new technique. In quilt guilds and sewing circles we share knowledge, so this can be an opportunity for quilters to make use of the expertise within the group to teach one another.

Note: Usually, when a group commits to making a quilt together each participant will purchase a copy of the pattern. For this quilt, we encourage you, and give permission, for copies of the templates and instructions to be distributed to group members from a single copy of the book (of course we also hope you love the book so much each person will want a copy for themselves!).

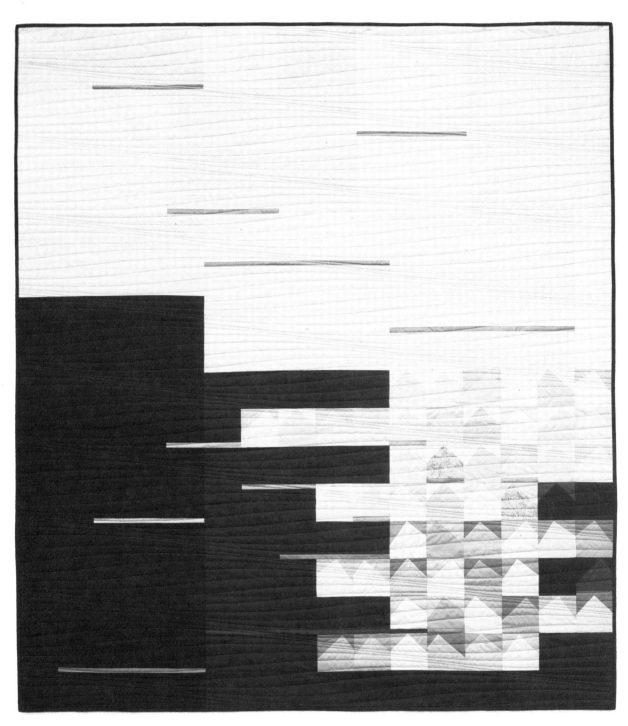

Corner Brook
2021
64" × 72" (163 cm × 183 cm)
Quilted by Amanda Nielsen

Working on a Group Quilt

Designing anything—a quilt, a building, a curriculum—involves setting parameters and then working within those parameters. When it comes to a group quilt such as *House*, you are designing a few aspects that come together for the whole: the quilt itself (object), a block/module for each individual quilter to contribute (exercise), and a process by which many people can participate (system). These aspects are interdependent; they are designed in concert with one another rather than separately.

1. OBJECT: THE QUILT

Begin by answering some basic questions: What is the overall vision for the quilt? What is its purpose—will it become a twin-sized quilt that is used at a local community shelter? Will it hang in a show and not necessarily have a functional use? Is there a theme that it aims to address—housing and shelter, food insecurity, colour exploration, a specific technique?

From there, you can begin to generate a design:

- Set the size of the quilt.
- Determine the size and total number of blocks.
- Determine the negative space that will be used around the blocks, if any. More traditional applications of negative space are sashing and borders. Alternate grids, like in the sample quilt for *House*, can be asymmetrical and free from repetition or regularity.
- Determine the overall colour scheme. Limiting the colour palette will contribute to a cohesive outcome.

2. EXERCISE: BLOCKS/MODULES

The focus of the block design is the individual quilters who will be working on the quilt. What are they willing to contribute, what do they already have on hand, and what skills do they already possess or want to learn?

- Determine a shape to be repeated within the blocks. Keeping to one shape makes it simple for everyone. See *Polygons in Squares* on page 110.
- Determine the size of the block. The unit size of the *House* blocks is 5" (12.5 cm) square (4½" [11.5 cm] square, finished). This size makes it easy to start with a charm square, a common pre-cut size, for those not using the improv method.
- Determine the skills required for the block. Alternatively, invite participants to expand their skillset by learning a new technique and provide support for them to do so.
- Set a rule about the colour placement within the block.
- If possible, keep the fabric selection broad. Allow for a variety of fabrics that people can find in their stashes.

Here are some of the things I have learned from being a participant in group quilts and from managing projects of my own.

- **Keep it simple.** If you're working with a group in which the participants aren't necessarily close friends or individuals you've worked with before, keep the design of the quilt simple. People will feel more comfortable joining in, and if someone needs to back out, their jobs or tasks can be taken on by someone else without too much trouble. Of course, if you are part of a bee group that has worked together for years and are familiar with the skills and styles of your peers and feel comfortable discussing more complex ideas with them, go for it.

- **Identify a leader.** A person needs to be identified and communicated as the leader of the project. In this way, instructions come from one place, tasks are tracked in one place, blocks are received by one person, and questions can be directed to one place. Support can be provided by others where needed, but having a single face of the project avoids confusion.

- **Be clear.** Communicate the instructions well. Delegate tasks to specific people and state clear timelines.

- **Give people choice.** In a professional setting, workers are often happier over the long term if they have some choice in what they do. Providing autonomy gives people freedom to choose. Quilters within a group will possess a variety of skills and interests. Some will prefer to stay within their comfort zone; others might be excited to venture into new-to-them territory. Some skills and equipment are more specialized (e.g., quilting with a computerized long-arm machine or custom quilting); some quilters might lack time but be willing to donate supplies such as batting or backing fabric. Providing different ways for people to participate opens the project up to more people.

Polygons in Squares

The idea behind the *House* block design is simple: a variety of irregular, five-sided shapes within a square, with right angles at the bottom corners. Offering three different methods of construction—traditional piecing, FPP, and improvisation—invites participants to do what they're comfortable with or branch out into a different technique using a very simple block.

When working with a group, setting parameters is imperative. For a cohesive outcome, there needs to be a set of rules to follow. The sample version of *House* has specific colour parameters:

- Use the given colour palette.
- Within each block, pair two colours of the same hue (e.g., pinks, oranges, blues) together, one light and one dark. Their value contrast can be high or low.
- Use solids, blenders, or small-scale tone-on-tone prints.

Colour placement can alter the essence of the quilt. This alternate version has the houses in white, with even larger swaths of negative space. See Figure 1.

You could use this general design idea with hexagons or octagons as well. See Figures 2 and 3.

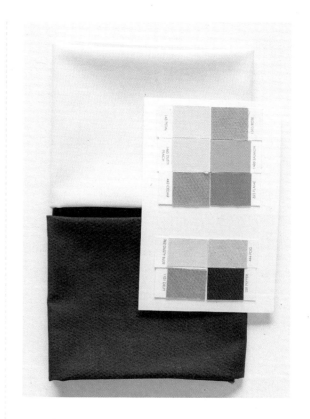

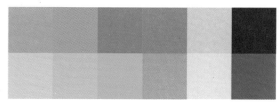

Providing both fabric and digital swatches that come from a line of fabric helps contributors select a unified palette from their stash.

Figure 1: Alternate colour placement of the *House* blocks.

Figure 2. Rows of irregular hexagons.

Figure 3: Rows of mixed regular and irregular octagons.

Making the *House* Blocks

HOUSE: TRADITIONAL PIECING

For each house, you will need the following:
- One 5" (12.5 cm) square for the house
- Two 2¾" (7 cm) squares for the background

Instructions

1. On the wrong side of the 2¾" (7 cm) squares, mark a diagonal line from corner to corner.
2. Align one of the smaller squares on the top-right corner of the 5" (12.5 cm) square, right sides together, with the line oriented as shown. Sew on the drawn line.
3. Trim off the corner, leaving a ¼" (6 mm) seam allowance. Press the seam toward the darker fabric.
4. Repeat with the second 2¾" (7 cm) square, aligning it with the top-left corner of the unit.

Note: If you are using a directional fabric, pay careful attention to the direction you mark and sew the diagonal.

HOUSE: FOUNDATION PAPER PIECING (FPP)

This pattern does not include instructions for FPP; however, there are many online tutorials, which you can find in the *Resources* section.

For each house, you will need the following:
- One 5" (12.5 cm) square for the house
- One 5" (12.5 cm) square for the background; cut in half on the diagonal

Instructions

1. Copy the templates from page 113 at 400% scale or download the templates at 3rdstoryworkshop.com/quilting-book#house and print at 100%. Check that the 1" (2.5 cm) test square actually measures that size when printed (adjust as needed if it doesn't).
2. Cut out the templates on the outside line, including the grey seam allowance.
3. Pre-fold the templates along the stitch lines before you begin.
4. Piece the template by paper piecing in the suggested order: House [1], Background [2], Background [3]. Make sure to use a shorter stitch length to make it easier to rip out the paper later.

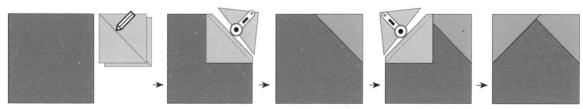

Traditional piecing

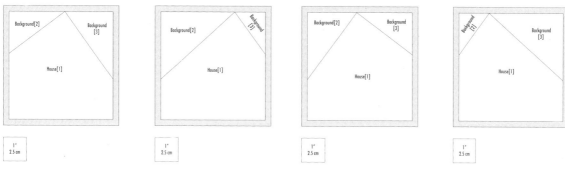

Photocopy these templates at 400% scale or download them at 3rdstoryworkshop.com/quilting-book#house. Grey indicates seam allowance.

5. Gently remove the paper from the back of the block. (You can also wait to remove the paper after the blocks have been pieced together. This can be especially helpful if you're working in a group and the blocks are being passed between members.)

Note: Because of its simplicity, this is a great pattern for freezer paper FPP; see the *Resources* section.

HOUSE: IMPROV

With this method, you will make two houses at a time. One will be the inverse of the other in terms of fabric placement.

For two houses, you will need the following:
- Two 7" (18 cm) squares

Instructions

1. Stack your two squares, right sides facing up.
2. With or without a ruler, slice off the top-right corner of the squares. The proportions are up to you—it can be a small corner, a big corner, a steep slope, or a gentle slope. See Figure 1.
3. Unstack the fabrics and pair the two corner pieces with their opposite fabric partner. See Figure 2.
4. For each unit, sew the corner to the house with a ¼" (6 mm) seam allowance, as shown in Figure 3a. Press the seam allowance toward the corner or press it open. Trim the excess fabric at the top of each unit. See Figure 3b.

5. Stack the two units again and cut off the top-left corners. The top point of your slice should roughly meet the peak of the house. The slope of this cut does not need to mirror the right side. See Figure 4.

6. Unstack the fabrics and pair the two corner pieces with their opposite fabric partner, as in Step 3.

7. For each unit, place the corner piece on the house, right sides together, with the top of the corner piece offset a ¼"

(6 mm), as shown in the diagram. You may find it helpful to mark the seam allowance on the wrong side of the corner piece to help align it correctly. Sew together with a ¼" (6 mm) seam allowance. Press the seam allowance toward the corner or press it open. See Figure 5.

8. Trim the units to 5" (12.5 cm) square, making sure to leave a ¼" (6 mm) seam allowance at the peak of the house. See Figure 6.

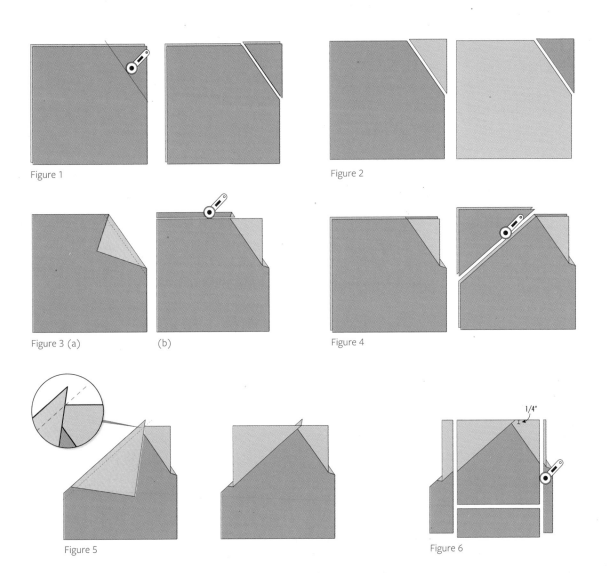

Figure 1

Figure 2

Figure 3 (a)   (b)

Figure 4

Figure 5

1/4"

Figure 6

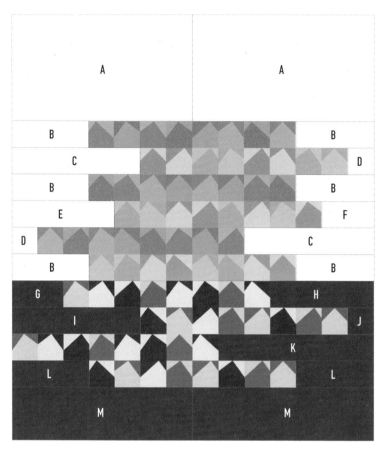

Layout diagram. You can use the web-based app PreQuilt to digitally mock up your own colours or insert your own block designs into the layout. See *Resources* or 3rdstorywork-shop.com/quilting-book#house.

Setting: Landscape

A *quilt setting* is how quilt blocks are arranged and sewn together into a quilt. Sometimes this is referred to as a *layout*.

The original version of this quilt was inspired by the landscape of a specific place—Corner Brook, Newfoundland—a small city nestled at the mouth of the Humber River and set against the mountainous landscape of the Humber Arm. *House* riffs on the same layout: a horizon line divides the quilt into asymmetrical proportions and organizes the blocks into warm and cool colour schemes with ample negative space around the houses.

The following are instructions to complete the quilt as in the sample.

Finished size: 63" × 72" (160 cm × 183 cm)

House **Blocks Required**
48 house blocks in warm colours
32 house blocks in cool colours

Fabric Requirements for Sample Setting/Layout
Sky Background: 1¾ yd (1.6 m)
Water Background: 1 yd (0.95 m)
Backing: 4 yd (3.7 m)[1]
Binding: ½ yd (0.45 m)

---

1   Backing amount is based on 42" (107 cm) of usable width with the seam running horizontally.

Cutting

Note: Use fabric with a minimum 42" (107 cm) width of fabric (WOF).

From the Sky fabric:

Cut two 18½" (47 cm) × WOF.

- A: Trim both strips to 18½" × 32" (47 cm × 81.5 cm)
- From the offcuts, sub-cut
  - E: (1) 5" × 18½" (12.5 cm × 47 cm)
  - F: (1) 5" × 9½" (12.5 cm × 24 cm)

Cut four 5" (12.5 cm) × WOF.

- From the first strip, cut
  - C: One 5" × 23" (12.5 cm × 58.5 cm)
  - B: One 5" × 14" (12.5 cm × 35.5 cm)
- Repeat with the second strip. Alternatively, stack the first two strips and cut them at the same time.
- From the third strip, cut
  - B: Two 5" × 14" (12.5 cm × 35.5 cm)
  - D: One 5" (12.5 cm) square.
- Repeat with the fourth strip. Alternatively, stack the third and fourth strips and cut them at the same time.

In total, from the four 5" (12.5 cm) × WOF strips, you should have six B, two C, and two D.

From the Water fabric:

Cut two 9½" (24 cm) × WOF.

- M: Trim both strips to 9½" × 32" (24 cm × 81.5 cm)

Cut three 5" (12.5 cm) × WOF.

- From the first strip, sub-cut
  - K: One 5" × 27½" (12.5 cm × 70 cm)
  - G: One 5" × 9½" (12.5 cm × 24 cm)
- From the second strip, sub-cut
  - I: One 5" × 23" (12.5 cm × 58.5 cm)
  - L: One 5" × 14" (12.5 cm × 35.5 cm)
- From the third strip, sub-cut
  - H: One 5" × 18½" (12.5 cm × 47 cm)
  - L: One 5" × 14" (12.5 cm × 35.5 cm)
  - J: One 5" (12.5 cm) square

Note: There are two L units, one cut from the second strip and one from the third.

From the Binding fabric:

Cut seven 2½" (6.5 cm) × WOF strips.

Assembly

Using a scant ¼" (6 mm) seam allowance,[2] sew the houses and pieces of landscape background, right sides together, into rows according to the layout diagram. Press as desired. Then, sew the rows together and press the seams open. Quilt as desired and finish the edge with 7 strips of 2½" (6.5 cm) × WOF binding.

---

2 A scant ¼" seam allowance is a seam allowance that is slightly narrower than ¼" inch. It compensates for the loss of some fabric in the folds of a seam, so that the dimensions of your block remain true once they are pressed. Find out more at 3rdstoryworkshop.com/tutorial-what-is-a-scant-1-4.

House taps into our collective power by using modularity, learning from other quilters, and working in a team to make a quilt together.

Repetition/Rhythm and Irregular Polygon. The repetition of the blocks lets each thrive in its uniqueness but sing together.

Warm/Cool Colours. The organization of the quilt into two sections highlights the interplay of warm and cool colours.

Asymmetry and Negative Space. This quilt was inspired by the landscape of a specific place. The division of the quilt into uneven portions with the horizon and the rows of houses being offset gives rise to movement and lends dynamism to the composition.

Solid/Print. Because the quilters in the group had different fabrics on hand, there is variation in the colours and the mix of solid and print fabrics. However, the limited colour palette brings unity to the quilt as a whole. ⧓

House
63" × 72" (160 cm × 183 cm)
Pieced by Eldora Baillie,
Melissa Christensen, Anja Clyke,
Dena Emeneau, Adrienne Klenck,
Barb Kulka, Gillian Noonan, Jeanette
Smith, Joanne Solak, Daphne
Themelis, and Andrea Tsang Jackson
Quilted by Nancy McDade,
Dream Weaver Custom Quilting

Quest No. 4
Era

QUEST: Capture a Moment in Time

> How can a quilt capture the feeling of an era?

History is a rich source of inspiration. Music, material culture, decor, pop culture, world events, notable figures, literature, and technology are all fodder for our design appetites. Shape, line, rhythm, texture, and more can emerge from these starting points.

First, I will walk you through my journey designing my own *Era: Boler* quilt inspired by a Boler camper (more on Bolers on page 120). From there, you have two choices:

Opposite:
Era: Boler
50" × 64"
(127 cm × 163 cm)
Quilted by
Carolyn Guy,
Whitney Oak Designs

1. Design your own *Era* blocks.

↓

1a. Incorporate your *Era* blocks into the general layout I designed.

2. Try my *Era: Boler* block using my improv curves technique.

↓

2a. Leave your *Boler* block(s) as is.

↓

2b. Incorporate your *Boler* blocks into the general layout I designed. *

* Going from 2 to 2b is essentially following a traditional pattern, which you are more than welcome to do.

QUEST MAP

Your journey through *Era* can meander, detour, or end where you want.

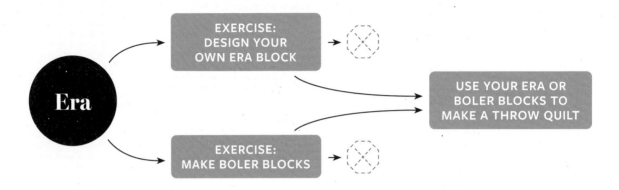

Curves & Time: Boler

The Boler is a small, lightweight travel trailer—also known as the "egg on wheels"—that was designed and manufactured in Winnipeg, Manitoba. About 10,000 units were sold between 1968 and 1988.[1] Bolers were constructed from two fibreglass-shell halves, which made for a durable and watertight trailer. The nature of the fibreglass material and manufacturing technology gave the trailer its smooth shape.

My friend Shehab spent over a year restoring an original Boler. He and his family wanted to decorate its interior in a manner that evoked the era that was the little trailer's heyday—the 1970s. They asked me to design and make a throw quilt for their new home on wheels.

The Bolers were all made with the top half in white and the bottom half in a single colour—most commonly a bright yellow or rich aqua blue. Today, the enamel paint with the right specifications only comes in a limited range of colours, and Shehab, in consultation with his family members, settled on a light blue. This piece of information, along with some other online Boler colour inspiration, gave me an entry point into the quilt design.

The next inspiration came from a photo he and his wife shared with me of a small 1970s kitchen vignette in which a mint green enamel pot sits atop a mustard stove. In addition, a quick Pinterest search for "'70s home decor" turned up some interesting wallpaper designs, with wide ovals in a regular geometric pattern; they looked like abstracted lanterns or pendant lamps that were popular in the period.

Concurrent with (but separate from) this conversation, I had been talking to Natalie Gerber, a surface pattern designer located across the country in Calgary, Alberta. I wanted to use some of her handprinted fabric

---

1   "History of the Boler," Boler-Camping, accessed August 22, 2024, https://www.boler-camping.com/portfolio/history-of-the-boler.

on a yet-to-be-decided project. We settled on a design that featured large-scale peonies, printed in four bold, warm inks on natural linen, as well as some linear, geometric patterns to complement.

The bright florals in warm colours turned out to be just the right tone for the Boler-era quilt. The background of the natural linen gave it an earthy feel, in contrast to the bright print. I pulled some solid and shot-cotton fabrics from my stash in more muted versions of Natalie's inks to highlight but also tone down the colours of her print.

The wallpaper patterns I had come across online had a similar shape to the Boler, although not as boxy. I fused the ideas of the Boler, wallpaper designs, and pendant lamps together, creating a design with two improvised curves nested into one another. A set of two mirrored curves would create a wide oval. The reversal of the colour placement in the top and bottom halves would speak to the halves of the Boler. I made a test block to make sure the curves weren't too tight to make.

After deciding on the curve blocks, I wanted the rest of the quilt to be simple in its geometry, creating a contrast. The rhythm of the strips of fabric is basic but asymmetrically borders the curved shapes to the left and right. The strips very abstractly represent the landscape elements the Boler travels through—horizontal, vertical, and climbing. They also have a verticality that contrasts the squat nature of the curved shapes.

There was no single starting point with this design; in fact, there may have been too many starting points—the Boler, the feature fabric, the wallpaper and lamps. The scale

and saturation of the handprinted fabric were well outside my comfort zone. The process of design is not often straightforward. For me, it starts with "bits" like these that aren't connected. It takes surrender and then practice to feel confident that all the bits will eventually come together.

Exercise: Design Your Own *Era* Block

In this exercise, you will choose a historical period and design a partial quilt inspired by that era. The partial quilt measures 16" × 48" (41 cm × 122 cm). This prescribed area can be made up of a single design that fills up the whole space, 3 or 12 square blocks, or 4 or 16 rectangular blocks.

The quilt can become a throw-sized quilt with the instructions that follow; don't get bogged down by this possibility for now, but keep it in the back of your mind.

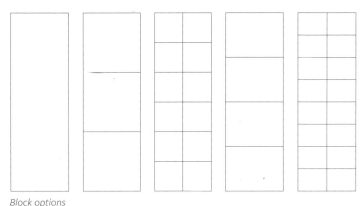

Block options
One 16" × 48" (40.5 cm × 122 cm) rectangle
Three 16" (40.5 cm) squares
Twelve 8" (20.5 cm) squares
Four 16" × 12" (40.5 cm × 30.5 cm) rectangles
Sixteen 8" × 6" (20.5 cm × 15 cm) rectangles

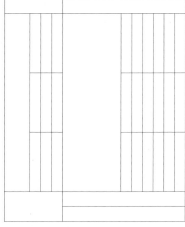

Expanded into throw quilt

CHOOSE AN ERA THAT INTERESTS YOU

It can be vague or specific—especially in its connection to a place. Think: New York City in the Jazz Age, Ancient Greece, Ming Dynasty, Gothic Rome, the 1990s.

ASK QUESTIONS

- What colours were popular during that time?
- What important events happened at that point in local or world history?
- How did people, both common and royal/wealthy, decorate their homes during that time?
- What music, fashion, and art emerged during that time?
- What movies have been made and what books have been written about the era?
- What technologies were new? Technology is tightly intertwined with design, and design gives rise to shapes and forms. New materials, new pigments, and new tools make for new possibilities. Material culture—that is, the physical stuff all around us—is an important indicator of what is manufactured by contemporary technologies. For example, the Space Race of the 1950s and 1960s inspired chrome colours and aerodynamic curves in design.

COLLECT VISUALS

Gather visuals from the answers to your questions. It can take a few minutes, a few days, or a few weeks (or even months or years) of collecting before inspiration strikes. Continue to be alert to prompts that could lead you down a rabbit hole of knowledge about the historical period and help you to add visual information—a podcast, a TV show, a postcard, an ad, a food, an antique, an item from the thrift shop, an abstract pattern from a mural that has just the right colour combination.

The easiest way to collect images digitally is on a Pinterest board. You may have already searched your era on Pinterest to find answers to the prompts above. But because our aim is to make a quilt—a tactile object—it will be useful to make a collection that you can touch. Print out a few choice images, gather ephemera, pull out fabrics from your stash. I like having the collection out for a stretch of time so I can stare at it or get glimpses of it while I go about my day.

START TO BUILD A LANGUAGE

Sorting and editing your visual findings is a key step. Whether you have gathered a little or a lot of inspiration, it is important to distill it into something cohesive.

○ What shapes and forms can be derived from your collection? Are there one or two shapes that you are curious about? Do you wonder if you can make those shapes in fabric? Set these aside.

A collection of inspirations: fabric swatches, photos, and the original upholstery from the Boler (top right).

○ What colour combinations evoke a sense of your era? If you see a repetition of colours or colour combinations that especially appeal to you, group them together.
○ What fabric substrates evoke that time? Are there textures that could help you select fabric for your quilt—shimmers, wovens, velvet, lace, a particular scale of floral print? Pull digital swatches or swatches from your stash.

Note: Keep the rest of the collection even after you narrow it down. You can always come back to it if you get stuck or need some fresh inspiration.

DETERMINE FORM(S)

Look at your shape inspiration. Are the forms based on a 90-degree shape, like a square or rectangle (or derivation thereof, like half-square triangles or other basic quilt block units)? Are they rooted in a 60-degree shape, like an equilateral triangle, a rhombus, or a hexagon? Or maybe they evoke some sort of irregular polygon or a series of curves?

> The process is not as linear as asking questions, finding answers, moving to visuals, then designing, choosing fabric, and making a quilt. There will be concurrent steps, backward steps, trying something in fabric, and circling back to ask more questions.

DESIGN

It's important that you know what you're getting yourself into before you commit to making a quilt of your own design. The following steps will guide you through the design process. However, there is always an out: once you get through these four steps, you can always discard what you have and return to Step 1, "Start small."

You will need a pen or pencil and some markers or coloured pencils. If you prefer to use digital tools, I suggest you use graphics software or the online app *PreQuilt.com*. PreQuilt is web-based software that helps quilters visualize and design quilts. The layout I designed for the *Era: Boler* quilt is also in PreQuilt; you can find it there and play around digitally with your block designs, then integrate them into the layout if you like. Find the links at 3rdstoryworkshop.com/quilting-book#era.

1. **Start small.** Make multiple copies of the layouts on page 125 and doodle around with a pencil. The subdivisions are there to help you break down the bigger blocks into smaller units that can be repeated, or they can be unique blocks if you like. It can be as simple as making half-square triangles with specific colour placements and sliding or rotating them.

2. **Get bigger.** Use the dotted grid of the design templates on page 126 to make larger versions of your block designs. Each space represents a 1" (2.5 cm) square. Include as much detail as you want.

3. **Draw at 1:1 scale.** Using quilting rulers and bigger paper, such as a pad of newsprint, draw the design at the final scale using one of the block sizes listed above, such as a 16" × 12" (40.5 cm × 30.5 cm) rectangle or 16" (40.5 cm) square. This will give you an idea of whether your fabrics (especially if they're prints) will work together. If you have fabric that you are willing to sacrifice, you may skip this step and go right to making a test block.

4. **Make a test block.** Make a full test block in the chosen size. Then, ask the following questions:

    ◎ Does the block start to capture the sense of the era?
    ◎ Does it achieve the effect you are seeking?
    ◎ Is the colour placement pleasing?
    ◎ Can you replicate it with relative ease?
    ◎ Is it fun to make?

    If the answers to these questions are yes, you are ready to commit to the design. If your answer to any of the questions is no, take a few steps back and try again. Ask yourself the following:

    ◎ What aspect of the era am I trying to capture?
    ◎ Can I change the colours, tones, or fabrics, while keeping the shapes, to achieve what I'm looking for?

    ◎ If I can't replicate the test block with relative ease, what notes should I take as I make my next test?
    ◎ If it isn't fun to make but checks all the other boxes, is it bearable to make just two or three more to complete the area? Or should I go back and design a different block or design the same block but construct it differently?

    Once you have answered the first set of questions in Step 4 adequately, make the number of additional blocks needed to fill the 16" × 48" (41 cm × 122 cm) (finished) area. You can quilt and bind it as is, add more blocks to make a bigger quilt, or use the layout later in this chapter to make a 50" × 64" (127 cm × 163 cm) throw quilt.

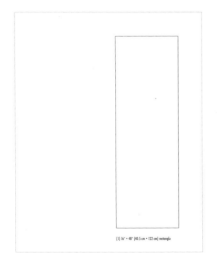
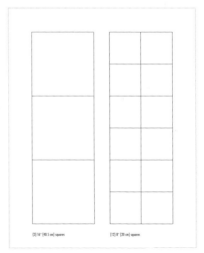
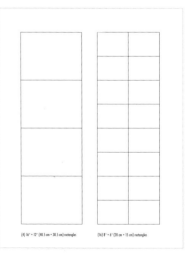

Era layout templates. Photocopy these at 500% scale for a full sheet or enlarge them at another scale. You can also download them at 3rdstoryworkshop.com/quilting-book#era.

Download these templates at 3rdstoryworkshop.com/quilting-book#era.
Note: The dots in these templates will not photocopy well. Use the download for printing instead.

PRACTICING SURRENDER

When it comes to designing your own *Era* block, your research may be all over the place at the beginning. You won't know how everything will converge. It takes surrendering to the process. It takes faith to trust that putting one foot in front of the other, even stepping backwards sometimes, is what you need to do, even if you don't know where you're going. Once you have some experience doing it, it gets easier—although not always comfortable—to feel confident that, without a laid-out path, all the bits that matter will eventually come together.

Exercise: Make *Boler* Blocks

This block, inspired by the Boler camper and the 1970s, is based on concentric improvised curves. Four units make up the quadrants of an oval. The finished block measures 16" × 12" (40.5 cm × 30.5 cm). If you have never made improvised curves before, consider making a test block with scrap fabrics from your stash before cutting into your final fabrics.

Fabric Requirements and Cutting for One Block

- Fabrics A and B: one fat eighth of each of fabric (a fat eighth measures 9" × 20" [23 cm × 51 cm]).
- From each fabric, cut two 10" × 8" (25.5 cm × 20.5 cm) pieces.

Other Supplies:

- Fabric glue pen
- Rotary cutter and cutting mat

Note: Use fabric with a minimum 42" (107 cm) width of fabric (WOF).

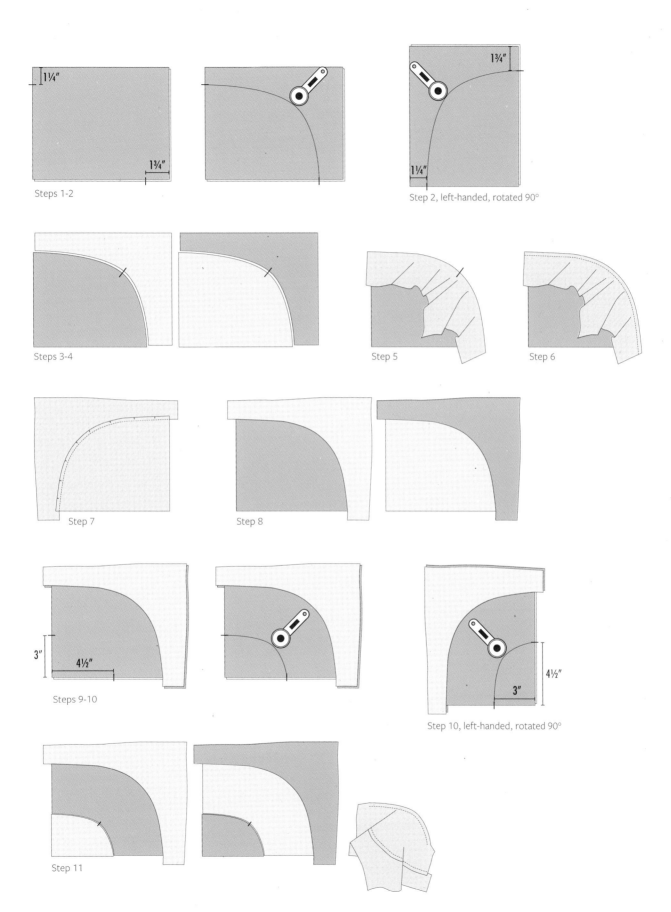

Steps 1-2

Step 2, left-handed, rotated 90°

Steps 3-4

Step 5

Step 6

Step 7

Step 8

Steps 9-10

Step 10, left-handed, rotated 90°

Step 11

Note: If you plan to incorporate these blocks into a throw quilt, you'll need to make a total of four blocks. You'll need a ½ yd (0.5 m) each of two fabrics (these will be Fabrics B and C in the throw quilt instructions; see page 130). From each fabric, cut the following, then proceed as instructed:

- Cut two 8" (20 cm) × WOF pieces.
  - Sub-cut eight 8" × 10" (20 cm × 25.5 cm) pieces.

Tips for Sewing Curves

- Take your time and go slowly.
- If your fabric is bunching, stop with your needle down, lift your presser foot, and adjust the fabric before continuing.

Instructions

1. With right sides up, stack one Fabric A rectangle on top of a Fabric B rectangle with the 10" (25.5 cm) side oriented horizontally. Set the other rectangles aside for now.
2. Make one mark roughly 1¾" (4.5 cm) in from the bottom-right corner and another mark roughly 1¼" (3 cm) down from the top-left corner.

If you're left-handed, you may want to rotate the unit counterclockwise 90 degrees so you can cut from the bottom mark up to the mark on the right side.

3. Freehand cut a curve from one mark to the other, starting at the bottom. Practice the motion a few times with your rotary cutter closed. You will have two quarter ovals and two curved L shapes. Pair each quarter oval with the L-shaped piece of the other fabric.
4. Take one set and mark both pieces at roughly the mid-point along the curve.
5. Place the L-shaped piece on top of the quarter-oval piece, right sides together. Glue baste the seam allowance in place, matching the marked mid-points and basting outward from there. Alternatively, carefully pin them in place. *Note:* The ends of the two curves will not meet up. The L-shaped piece will extend beyond the quarter-oval piece, as shown in the diagram.
6. Sew along the curve using a ¼" (6 mm) seam allowance.
7. Snip ⅛" (3 mm) into the seam allowance along the curve to ease the fabric. Press the seam allowance toward the darker fabric.
8. Repeat Steps 4–7 with the second pair of cut shapes.
9. Stack the two units on top of each other again, right sides up, lining up the bottom-left corners of the quarter-oval shapes.
10. Make one mark roughly 4½" (11.5 cm) in from the bottom-left corner and another mark roughly 3" (7.5 cm) up from the bottom-left corner. As with Step 2, if you're left-handed, you may want to rotate the unit counterclockwise 90 degrees so you can cut from the bottom mark up to the mark on the right side.

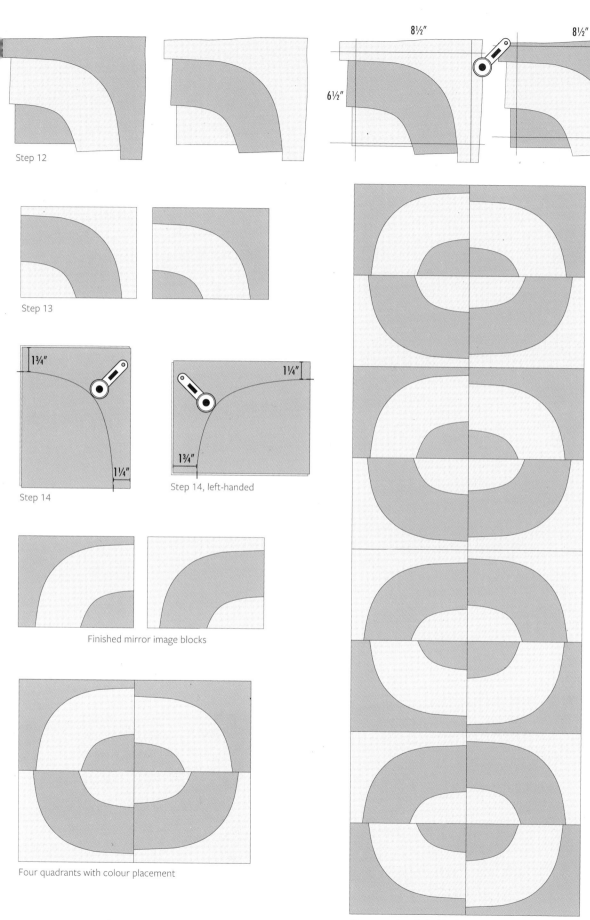

Step 12

8½"   8½"

6½"   6½"

Step 13

1¾"   1¼"
              1¾"
       1¼"

Step 14   Step 14, left-handed

Finished mirror image blocks

Four quadrants with colour placement

Four complete *Boler* blocks

11. Freehand cut a curve from one mark to the other, starting at the bottom. This second cut will be roughly parallel to the first curve. Pair each inner quarter oval with the opposite pieced L shape so the fabrics alternate.

12. Repeat Steps 4–7 with the sub-units from Step 11.

13. Trim each unit to 8½" × 6½" (21.5 cm × 16.5 cm). For variety, centre the trim differently for each unit.

14. Using the remaining two Fabric A and B rectangles, repeat Steps 1–13 but in the mirror image to make the remaining two units of the final block. To make the improvised cut in Step 1 easier, orient your stacked rectangles with the 10" (25.5 cm) side oriented vertically (right-handed) or horizontally (left-handed).

15. Arrange the four units as shown, matching the outside fabrics for the top and bottom halves of the block. Using a scant ¼" (6 mm) seam allowance,[2] sew the units together into rows. Press as desired. Then, sew the rows together and press the seams open. *Note:* Be sure to use a scant ¼" (6 mm) seam allowance when assembling the blocks to ensure your block will be the correct size when you're finished.

If you enjoyed making this block and would like to continue to make the throw quilt, repeat this process to make a total of four *Boler* blocks with the remaining 8" × 10" (20 cm × 25.5 cm) rectangles.

Use Your *Era* or *Boler* Blocks to Make a Throw Quilt

You can take your finished *Era* or *Boler* blocks a step further and incorporate them into a throw-size quilt that measures 50" × 64" (127 cm × 163 cm). A simple pieced border at the top and bottom and chunky vertical strips frame the 16" × 48" (41 cm × 122 cm) partial quilt created by your *Era* or *Boler* blocks.

Mod Fire, a three-colour, slightly elaborated version of this design—in cobalt blue, hot pink, and beige—is shown at the beginning of the *Atlas* section of this book (see page 74). The instructions below will make a quilt in the same layout as my finished *Boler* quilt but using only three colours, like *Mod Fire*. Feel free to substitute additional fabrics if you desire the scrappier feel of my *Boler* quilt. The fabric requirements do not account for the already pieced *Era* or *Boler* blocks that will make up the main column.

To help you visualize your layout, you can use the web-based app PreQuilt to create a digital mockup: 3rdstoryworkshop.com/quilting-book#era.

Finished size: 50" × 64" (127 cm × 163 cm)

Era or *Boler* **Blocks Required**

Four *Boler* blocks, sewn together in a vertical arrangement, or your own design measuring 16½" × 48½" (42 cm × 123 cm), unfinished

---

2   A scant ¼" seam allowance is a seam allowance that is slightly narrower than one ¼" inch. It compensates for the loss of some fabric in the folds of a seam, so that the dimensions of your block remain true once they are pressed. Find out more at 3rdstoryworkshop.com/tutorial-what-is-a-scant-1-4.

Fabric Requirements for Setting/Layout

Fabric A (Feature): ⅞ yd (0.8 m)

Fabric B (Accent): ⅞ yd (0.8 m)[3]

Fabric C (Background): 1¼ yd (1.15 m)[3]

Backing[4]: 3¼ yd (3 m)

Binding: ½ yd (0.5 m)

Fabric A, Feature

Fabric B, Accent

Fabric C, Background

Cutting

WOF = Width of fabric, assuming a minimum 42" (107 cm) usable width

From Fabric A (Feature):

Cut one 16½" (42 cm) × WOF strip.

- Sub-cut nine 16½" × 3½" (42 cm × 9 cm) strips.

Cut two 4½" (11.5 cm) × WOF strips.

- Trim to two 4½" × 34½" (11.5 cm × 87.5 cm) strips.

From Fabric B (Accent):

Cut one 16½" (42 cm) × WOF strip.

- Sub-cut nine 16½" × 3½" (42 cm × 9 cm) strips.

Cut one 8½" (21.5 cm) × WOF strip.

- Sub-cut two 8½" × 16½" (21.5 cm × 42 cm) rectangles.

From Fabric C (Background):

Cut one 16½" (42 cm) × WOF strip.

- Sub-cut nine 16½" × 3½" (42 cm × 9 cm) strips.

Cut two 4½" (11.5 cm) × WOF strips.

- Trim to two 4½" × 34½" (11.5 cm × 87.5 cm) strips.

Cut two 7½" (19 cm) × WOF strips.

- Trim to two 7½" × 24½" (19 cm × 62 cm) rectangles.

From the Binding:

Cut seven 2½" (6.5 cm) × WOF strips.

---

3 If you're making the quilt using the *Boler* blocks (and not your own *Era* design), this amount is in addition to the ½ yd (0.50 m) of these fabrics you used to make the *Boler* blocks.

4 Backing amount is based on 42" (107 cm) of usable width with the seam running horizontally. Less fabric could be used if the backing is pieced with additional scraps.

Assembly

Use a scant ¼" (6 mm) seam allowance to assemble the quilt top.

1. **Vertical strips** (Figure 1): Gather all the 3½" × 16½" (9 cm × 42 cm) strips. Sew the strips into sets of three as shown, pressing the seam allowance in the direction indicated. You will have a total of nine of these units, three of each fabric arrangement.

2. **Top and bottom borders** (Figure 2):
   a. Sew a 4½" × 34½" (11.5 cm × 87.5 cm) Fabric A rectangle to the top of a 4½" × 34½" (11.5 cm × 87.5 cm) Fabric C rectangle. Press the seam allowance to one side.
   b. Sew a 16½" × 8½" (42 cm × 21.5 cm) Fabric B rectangle to the left side of the strip unit as shown. Make sure Fabric A is at the top of the strip unit. Press away from Fabric B.
   c. Repeat Steps 2a–2b to create a second border unit.

3. **Left background border**: Sew the 7½" × 24½" (19 cm × 62 cm) Fabric C rectangles together along one short end. Press the seam allowance to one side.

4. Assemble the quilt as shown in Figure 3, pressing the seam allowances in the directions indicated.
   a. Begin by sewing the vertical strip units into three columns of three units each.

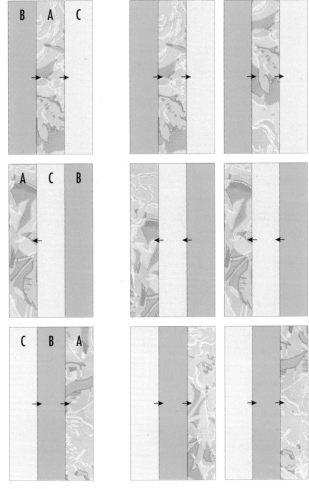

Figure 1

   b. Next, sew the middle columns (left background border, three vertical-strip columns, and your feature-block column) together.
   c. Finally, add the top and bottom borders.

5. To finish the quilt, quilt as desired and finish the edge with seven strips of 2½" (6.5 cm) × WOF binding.

Figure 2

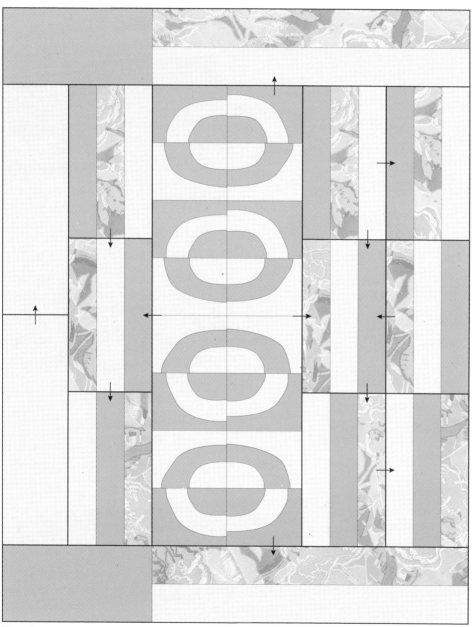

Figure 3

ELEMENTS OF *ERA*

Building Containers. I built you a container that was the size of a throw quilt. Within it, you had the freedom to do what you wanted with a 16" × 48" (41 cm × 122 cm) area, including filling it in with the improvised curve blocks I designed. Even smaller still were the containers of three or more blocks that could be used to fill the area.

In the design process, you started with sketches that were small, then grew them to scale. Paper is much less risky than fabric—easily acquired and recycled if it doesn't turn out right. Making one test block is a small commitment of time and fabric.

Symmetry/Asymmetry. The feature blocks (the *Boler* blocks or the *Era* blocks of your own design) are offset to the side. The strips to the left and right of the feature blocks are not symmetrical in design or proportion. Top to bottom along a horizontal axis, the design is proportionally symmetrical, but the fabric placement is not, most notably at the top and bottom "borders," which are repeated rather than mirror images of each other. To me, the asymmetry represents the chaos of nature that surrounds the trailer.

Scale. Natalie's fabric designs are intended for home decor—drapes, cushion covers, and such. Home-decor prints can be big because the fabrics are used in large swaths and the repeat pattern can be seen and admired from afar. Quilting cottons, on the other hand, are designed and printed at a smaller scale so that they will read well when they are cut up and pieced. I had to come to terms with the fact that Natalie's peonies would be chopped up. The blocks and pieces of fabric are quite chunky in this quilt design to preserve some of the floral motif; the smallest finished dimension of fabric is 3" (7.5 cm) wide. The curved Boler motifs were scaled accordingly, so they would remain the focal point of the quilt as a whole, even with a bold and colourful print.

Improvisation and Curves. Within the bounds of a rectangle, I have used concentric improvised curves as a reference to the Boler's distinct rounded-but-boxy shape.

Geometric Contrast and Rhythm /Repetition. In contrast to the improvised curves, the rest of the quilt is very structured and simple in its geometry, abstractly representing the landscape elements the Boler travels through. The rhythm of white strips climbs up and to the right. The strip sets asymmetrically flank the Boler shapes to the left and right, and they possess a verticality that contrasts the squat nature of the curved shapes.

Featured fabric:
Handprinted linen by Natalie Gerber:
- *FLORALZ* Collection: *Peoniez*
- *LOTSA* Collection: *Little Lines, Long Lines*

Small print:
Flowerland by Melody Miller, Ruby Star Society
Binding:
Birthday by Sarah Watts, Ruby Star Society

Mix of Textures. Floral and geometric prints and solids are combined. The solids give some respite from the large, loud print. The fibres are also mixed: handprinted natural linen, a commercial print at a small scale, shot cottons, and solid fabrics lend a varied texture, both visually and tactilely.

Colour Saturation. The source fabric contained four very bright inks on natural linen. These colours set the palette for my quilt. I mixed in some more muted tones of the brights—a tan, a more muted aqua green, and some off-white—to highlight the "climbing" motion of the stripes. ⏳

Quest No. 5
Fogo II

QUEST: Explore Place & Subvert Tradition

> How can I make a quilt that evokes my memory and experience of a specific place?
>
> Side Quest: How can tradition be subverted or "turned inside out?"

QUEST MAP

Your journey through *Fogo II* can meander, detour, or end where you want.

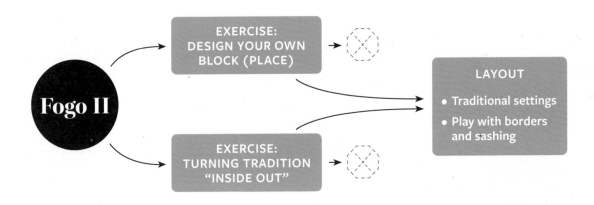

Place & Tradition

In Surrender (page 42), I shared my experience visiting a magical place—and the quilt that brought about that trip. On Fogo Island, Newfoundland, quilting is a significant craft, and there is a vibrant community of quilters making and selling quilts.

The Fogo Island Inn is a five-star resort at the centre of the island's rejuvenation effort, and although it is contemporary and minimal in a lot of ways, its design and decor are rooted in the traditional construction and craft of the area.

Some of the inn's walls are covered with custom-designed wallpaper—reminiscent of a bygone era or remote place but reimagined by a contemporary designer. Others are covered from floor to ceiling with shiplap that's been painted white, giving the interior a rustic and homey feel. These horizontal wooden slats come from a method of shipbuilding in which the wood is cut with a groove along its length so that the next piece tucks under, creating an overlap that protects the structure from the elements, including direct contact with the ocean's waters. The harsh climate of the region, on the North Atlantic's edge with its intense wind, water, salt, snow, and sleet, required this type of seal, and the method's simplicity made it ubiquitous for building exteriors. The shiplap's application inside,

Traditional quilt blocks of Fogo Island.

sometimes in its traditional horizontal orientation and sometimes turned vertically, is an aesthetic nod to the area's history.

Every bed in the inn is covered with a handmade quilt sewn by a local quilter. Different styles of blocks are common on the island, but they are unified by their wild scrappiness and exuberant colours. I have come to embrace these unique patterns, as well as the patterns that are more ubiquitous in quilting language but are, on Fogo Island, named in a specific "local quilting dialect:"

⊚ Heritage Hexagon
⊚ Seven-Pointed Star
⊚ Strip Quilts (String blocks)
⊚ Compass Points
⊚ Tea Leaf
⊚ Four-Pointed Star
⊚ Rob Peter to Pay Paul
⊚ Crazy Quilt (or Patch Quilt)

String blocks were, to my eye, the most common and used in so many different layouts (called "settings" in quilt-speak): diamonds, chevrons, laid in a checker pattern with large plain squares, sashed and bordered within a sampler. During my visit, I slept under a colourful string quilt made by local quilter Carolyn Harnett in 2017. Out on an excursion to the nearby town of Tilting, I visited the local quilt shop and met a few of the quilters who made these quilts.

When I came home from my trip, I had in mind that I wanted to make a string quilt inspired by my time on Fogo. As a modern quilter, I am most consistently inspired by traditional quilt patterns but want to put

Andrea's room at the Inn.

my own spin on them. There are a thousand different ways to do that—playing with the scale of the blocks, interrupting their regular patterns with new elements, allowing lots of negative space around them—the list is as long as our imaginations can stretch.

Because I was there during pack-ice season, there were different shades of white all around me. The gleaming white of the sun on floating ice, the aqua white of the ocean's pack ice as it smashed into the rocky shore, the cool purple-ish white of the small iceberg parked in view of the hotel room at dawn, the warm white of the late-morning sun on a frozen lake that we crossed.

String quilts are traditionally a way to use scraps of fabrics. Because of the strings' diagonal arrangement, the scraps can be all different lengths. They are pieced onto a foundation square—often discarded papers such as phone books or newsprint, which are ripped out after the block is complete, or sometimes an old sheet, which stays permanently on the back of the block.

The Fogo Island-inspired quilt I designed is about turning traditions inside-out—not to subvert them but to honour them in their uniqueness while bringing my own experiences to them. One of my natural aesthetic tendencies is to work with shades of white; as a result, I have a lot of white and off-white scraps sitting around. For this quilt, I wanted to use scraps of white to "subdue" some of the prints and colours in my stash.

The colour palette in paint chips and fabric swatches, with test string blocks. The palette is inspired by Fogo Island Workshops's furniture colours.

Exercise: Design Your Own Block

This exercise is similar to designing the *Era* block, but it differs in that it is personal. It is also more open-ended in terms of the finished size. Your research does not have to include external sources. You are the primary source, the object of the interview, the lens through which a place is recorded and remembered.

CHOOSE A PLACE

To begin, pick a place that is meaningful to you, that brings positive memories and feelings to mind.

ASK QUESTIONS

- What important people in your life do you associate with the place?
- How did you feel when you were there? Loved, expansive, small (in a good way), in awe?
- What did it feel like physically? Cool, dewy air in the morning, water running over your skin, incredible warmth in the dead of winter?
- What did it smell like? Salty air, freshly baked cookies, a hint of must, hay, dust, campfire?
- Were you there on a regular basis, or did you just visit one time?
- In your memory, how was the place lit? Sunshine, fireplace, a side-table lamp, dappled sunlight through the trees?
- What was the ambience like? Cozy, bright, intimate, spacious, spectacular?
- What sounds do you remember hearing? Specific music, chirping birds, children laughing, lapping waves?
- What colours do you associate with this place? A perfect sunset, a tile backsplash, a wall colour, your grandfather's favourite chair?
- Do you associate any tastes with this place? A regional dish, your favourite food that your grandma always made you, Christmas dinner, birthday cake, wine, salt on your lips after a dip in the ocean?
- Are there specific objects or things that remind you of this place? The colour of the stove, a quilt, a wooden spoon, a souvenir from a trip?

COLLECT EPHEMERA

- **Photos.** This is probably the easiest way to jog your memory. Maybe you have a million pictures of this place on your phone or just one precious photo from decades ago. Pick a selection of no more than five photos, the ones that answer the above questions in the most meaningful way.
- **Souvenirs and heirlooms.** Objects hold a lot of meaning, whether it's a precious ring, a tchotchke from a trip, or a birthday cake plate that was used every year.
- **Paper ephemera.** Hand-written cards, postcards, a program or ticket from an event—these objects help us remember events, people, and places. Letter mail that comes from a certain place or person helps us remember somewhere. Like photos, postcards we have picked up as souvenirs help us recall the feeling of a place.
- **Colour.** Go to the hardware store and choose paint chips that remind you of your place. Alternatively, look at your fabric stash and pull swatches from there.

START TO BUILD A LANGUAGE

This step is very much the same as the approach to the *Era* designs. Sort and edit your collection of ephemera to distill it into something cohesive.

- What shapes and forms can be derived from the collection? Are there one or two shapes that you are curious about? A coastline, a door handle, a decorative plate...Do you wonder if you can make those shapes in fabric?
- What colour combinations evoke a sense of your place?
- Are there textures that can inform the fabric selection for your quilt? A wallpaper print, a crochet blanket, dense foliage, a clear open sky?

DETERMINE FORM(S)

Look at your shape inspiration. Are the shapes based on a 90-degree shape, like a square or rectangle (or derivation thereof, like half-square triangles or other basic quilt block units)? Are they rooted in a 60-degree shape, like an equilateral triangle, a rhombus, or a hexagon? Or maybe they evoke some sort of irregular polygon or a series of curves?

DESIGN

You will need a piece of paper, a pen or pencil, and some markers or coloured pencils.

- Using your inspiration, draw a large shape almost filling the page. It can be abstract or figurative, but it shouldn't be too detailed. Repeat until you feel like you have something you want to explore further.
- Scale it or break it down.
  a. **Do you want this shape to be the basis of a set of repeated blocks?** You can capitalize on the modularity of traditional quilting. Download and print a dotted grid paper (square or triangular, depending on your shape): 3rdstoryworkshop.com/quilting-book#grid-papers. Using the grid as a guide, draw an outline of a block—it can be square, rectangular, triangular, or hexagonal. Redraw your shape inside that block. You can further subdivide your shape to add intricacy. Repeat the shape in adjacent "blocks."
  b. **Do you want it to be a large shape made up of smaller blocks?** Download and print a dotted grid paper: 3rdstoryworkshop.com/quilting-book#grid-papers. Trace or redraw your shape onto the grid. Using the dots, draw a grid on top of your shape, breaking down the line into units.

Make multiple attempts at this step, if necessary. Design is an iterative process, and quantity produces quality.

INTRODUCE PARAMETERS

Now it's time to make some rules around your shape.

- Experiment with colour placement. With your determined colour palette in mind, make a rule or set of rules about how the colour will be placed. For example, if your shape divides a square block into two unequal parts horizontally, the top must be colour and the bottom must be neutral.
- Play with the shape. Does it have to be exactly the same in every block, or can it vary slightly from block to block?
- Expand the negative space. Alternate your block design with empty space or add sashing between some or all of the blocks.
- Determine the method of construction: traditional piecing, improvisation, or appliqué.
- Determine the size of your block. Keep in mind that the method of construction may limit how big or small you can easily make your block.
- Determine the rough size of your finished quilt. This may send you back to re-determine the size of your block.

When you follow your parameters, it gives a sense of order. Because you've built modules, there is a sense of rhythm.

MAKE A TEST BLOCK

This step is, again, the same as designing your own *Era* block.

Make a full test block. Then, ask the following questions:

- Does the block start to capture the sense of your place?
- Does it achieve the effect you are seeking?
- Is the colour placement pleasing?
- Can you replicate it with relative ease?
- Is it fun to make?

If your answer to all these questions is yes, you are ready to commit to this design. If your answer to any of these questions is no, take a few steps back and try again. Ask yourself the following:

- What specific feeling or memory am I trying to capture?
- Can I change the colours, tones, or fabrics, while keeping the shapes, to achieve what I'm aiming for?
- If I make more test blocks, varying the colour placement, will the effect be different as a series of blocks? (If so, make more test blocks.)
- If I can't make the block again easily, what notes should I take as I make my next test block?
- If it isn't fun to make but checks all the other boxes, should I go back and design a different block or design the same block but construct it differently? Or is it bearable enough to push through and make the number of blocks needed for the quilt?

Once you have answered the first set of questions adequately, make the number of additional blocks needed to create the quilt. Add borders, sashing, or negative space as desired. The idea of this quilt is for it to be a sort of embodiment of the place that you remember, a symbol of it that lives outside your mind.

Exercise: Turning Tradition "Inside Out"

What was a bit simple, but also difficult, about a Fogo-inspired quilt was that quilting is important to the culture and that was part of what I found inspirational. Could I make a quilt about quilts and make it seem fresh? It seemed a bit circular. What I saw was an opportunity—like that of the architect, designers, and craftspeople who helped create the Fogo Island Inn—to revisit traditions and make them my own. Connecting the past to the present in this way is by no means a novel idea. It even gives rise to a whole category of quilts called "modern traditionalism."

My idea for turning traditional string blocks "inside out"—covering up carefully selected colours and prints with white fabrics—was a bit absurd. However, I wanted to see if the bit of translucency that white fabrics possess could tint each block. I didn't find the experiment terribly successful; the colours underneath weren't strong enough, and the whites weren't translucent enough or too tinted themselves for the colour to come through. However, the feeling of pack-

ice season did come through. Floating ice, glimpses of the churning water, and white on white on white were captured in the way these string blocks were coming together. I also loved the rhythmic way they are assembled.

For this exercise, is there a traditional quilt block that has always appealed to you? Do any of them speak to you about a meaningful place or memory? What can you do to the block to turn its traditional design "inside out" and make it yours?

Here is a list of traditional quilt blocks to get you started:

- Ohio Star
- Sawtooth Star
- Friendship Star
- Log Cabin
- Rail Fence
- Flying Geese
- Orange Peel
- Bear Paw

In this chapter, I do not provide instructions on how to make any of these traditional blocks or the string blocks[1] I used in my own quilt. A quick online search will yield many tutorials and patterns to guide you through the basic dimensions and proportions of the blocks. From there, you can start to turn them inside out. I've pulled some *Elements* from the list at the beginning of this *Atlas* (page 72) that you can use to play with and to tweak these traditional designs.

---

[1] A great string quilt tutorial can be found on Emily Dennis's blog: https://www.quiltylove.com/the-scrappy-and-happy-string-quilt/.

Ohio Star

Sawtooth Star

Friendship Star

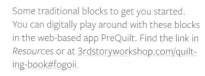

Some traditional blocks to get you started. You can digitally play around with these blocks in the web-based app PreQuilt. Find the link in *Resources* or at 3rdstoryworkshop.com/quilt-ing-book#fogoii.

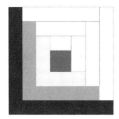
Log Cabin

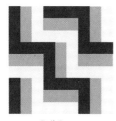
Rail Fence

Flying Geese

Orange Peel

Churn Dash

Bear Paw

Colour. Can you turn the colour saturation up or down? Go really bright or really neutral?

Value. Can you turn up the contrast between the units that make up the block? Or make them very low contrast?

Scale. Can you make the block very large, as big as a whole quilt, or very tiny, as small as a fingernail?

Line. Can you outline the shape of the block using the techniques from *Trellis*?

Negative Space. Can you surround the block with lots of negative space so it can really shine?

Irregular Polygons. Can you make the block out of improvised shapes that aren't perfect?

Texture. Can you use a linen/cotton blend or unconventional materials, such as silk, satin, lace, or table linens?

Appliqué or Reverse Appliqué. Can you take a traditionally pieced block and reconstruct it using appliqué or, for a bigger stretch, reverse appliqué (as in *Still Life*)?

As always in this process, build yourself a container by making a test block and starting with scraps or fabrics you already have in your stash. You can then build on the test block by making multiples or trying the same transformation on a different block.

For my string blocks, I wanted to use some fat quarters from my stash for my foundation blocks. Out of a fat quarter, I could comfortably cut four squares measuring 8½" (21.5 cm) each. (A fat quarter measures roughly 18" × 20" [45.5 cm × 51 cm.]) I could have made the string blocks in any dimension, but my decision was informed by the given dimensions of a fat quarter. What practical constraints can help you determine the way you use size or colour?

Elements can also be used to manipulate the traditional structures of a quilt: sashing, borders, and cornerstones.

Value and Contrast. Can you have these structures really blend in with the blocks? Or make them really bright with muted blocks? Light sashing with dark blocks or vice versa?

Scale and Negative Space. Can you make the structures very wide or extremely narrow? Or have none at all?

Shape. Can you piece other shapes into the sashing, cornerstones, and/or borders? Diamonds, Xs, flying geese?

Texture. Can you use a linen/cotton blend or unconventional materials, such as silk, satin, lace, or table linens?

From these exercises, you will create your own quilting "dialect," riffing on tradition. This is how we build the future of quilting and connect to its past. In Essay No. 5, we explored the collective power of quilting. I really do see our quilting ancestors and descendants as part of our community. We speak the same language but with different catchphrases, slang, and neologisms. I am connected to the quilters of Fogo Island in a new and intimate way because of our shared language.

ELEMENTS OF *FOGO II*

Colours. The quilt primarily uses neutral whites in a variety of shades with pops of colour. A range of saturation is included in the foundation blocks.

Rhythm and Movement. The repetitive internal structure of the string blocks themselves, as well as their repeated arrangement, gives the sense of a regular rhythm, as does the way the coloured stripes direct your eyes to the right and left.

Texture. The strings are made of quilting cotton as well as printed linen, cotton, and hemp scraps. These mixed natural fibres were handprinted by two Canadian textile designers: Alissa Kloet of Keephouse (Seaforth, Nova Scotia) and Jenna Fenwick of Jenna Rose (Mississippi Station, Ontario). The white linens have a larger weave and allow the foundation fabric to show a little more in some places.

The number of layers in the quilt differs across the quilt. The string blocks are sewn on an extra layer of fabric, which affects the drape of the quilt, making it heavier in some rows than others.

Opposite:
Fogo II
64" × 78½" (163 cm × 199 cm)

Line, Contrast, and Asymmetry. The stark line in the middle of the quilt is a direct reference to the wall hooks in my room at the inn. In the quilt, the off-black stripe grounds the white floating elements, interrupting the rhythm of the white and dividing the whole quilt unequally in two.

Negative Space. The sashing between the blocks is only horizontal, separating the blocks into rows and refers to the historic use of shiplap and its use at the Fogo Island Inn. ✕

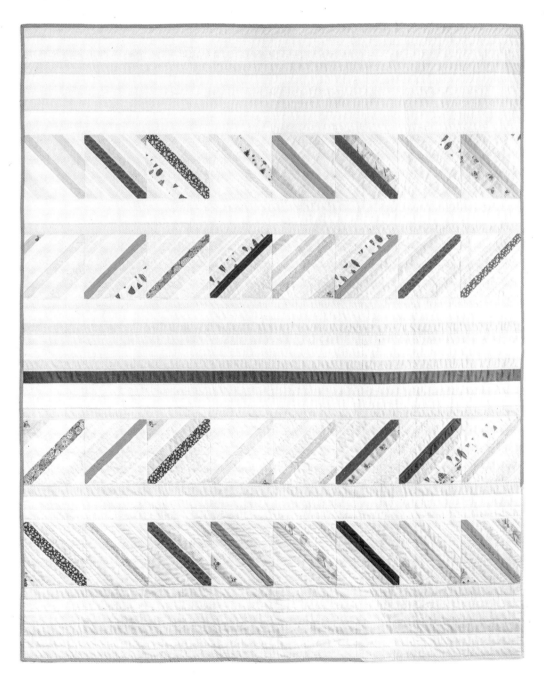

Conclusion

My goal with this book is to help quilters like you design your own creative journey—with attention and intention. I have invited you to think about why you make, how you make, and how to get more out of it—whether it's in the realm of actual making or in service of the other parts of your life. I have brought you along on my own quests; hopefully you've seen yourself reflected in them or discovered something new about yourself while touring with me. You may have disliked parts of it or disagreed with my premises and frameworks, but in those cases, I hope that you were able to appreciate where our different perspectives come from and understand that our different approaches make our craft broader, better, and stronger.

I hold many aspirations for you and for me as quilters:

- That quilting helps us gain insights into ourselves and how we relate to other people.
- That we have a sense of quilting's role in our lives, whether it grounds us in a very deep way or simply brings us joy.
- That we have a better idea how to tackle a new idea, skill, or even responsibility—one manageable bit at a time.
- That we test our ideas and discard them or persist at them if they don't quite work the way we imagined they would, both within our creative practices and outside of them.

- That however important quilting is to us, we don't hold on to it possessively but rather hold it loosely in our hands.
- That when we let go of control of the processes and outcomes, we will experience something new that we couldn't have orchestrated for ourselves.
- That we know that practicing our craft is the responsible thing to do—for ourselves and everyone around us.
- That we feel connected to a community of quilters—here and now, before and after us—if not in actuality, then at the very least in theory.

Where Do We Go from Here?

The idea of language and translation has recurred over the course of these essays and quests. We've discussed language in the literal sense—words to describe elements of quilting. And in another sense, I have invited you build your own quilting vocabulary through what we've done here—to express your creativity and ideas through the craft. I have taken you on some adventures to search for answers to questions about translating approaches across disciplines—design, drawing, painting. My own artistic explorations in the last few years have sparked these types of inquiries. This broad notion of quilting as a language, planted in my head by my mentor Frances Dorsey, will no doubt continue to fuel my next quests.

But where will *you* go next?

- What quests of your own do you want to pursue?
- What tools will you need?
- What small explorations might help you get there?
- What will you let go of?
- Who do you want around you? Will you need their support or will you support them?

Your creativity in quilting can take you to many different places—both literal (in a geographical sense), and within the space of your practice. You may already have a great sense of adventure when it comes to your craft, or you may be on the cusp of stepping outside of your comfort zone. When you open yourself up to possibilities, the sense that anything is possible can be daunting. I hope the tools I have given you can mitigate that particular overwhelm and help you forge ahead on a journey that is rewarding and fosters self-discovery.

When you're out there adventuring, you may sometimes feel that you've really achieved what you set out to do and may even receive the approval of your peers. You may sometimes feel that you've failed miserably in your efforts and fallen short of your own expectations. You may step away from the craft for a while or take it around a sharp turn in another direction. In any of these cases, quilting will always welcome you home. Let it be a place of refuge and a life-giving source.

Acknowledgments

A project like this takes many hands and hearts, and consequently, many thanks are due:

To my editor Kim Werker, who was always out on a limb with me and never talked me out of anything. After reading the first draft of the first chapter of this book, you told me that my writing voice is like my aesthetic voice—crisp and minimal. It gave me the confidence to see this book project through to the very end.

To Lisa Friesen of Ninth and May Design Co. for bringing everything together in concert. From the beginning, you had a sense of who I am as an artist and designer and you brought it out in every corner of the book's design.

To the editorial team: copyeditor Michelle Woodvine and technical editor Jessica Schunke, for helping me say what I mean and for thoroughly understanding and catching all the bits.

To my photographer, co-stylist, friend, and pretzel provider, Shaeline Stromberg, for bringing my quilt photography dreams to life. Your work is an expression of your deep-seated sense of home, hospitality, and welcome; I always feel it when I'm with you.

To my guildmates and friends: Eldora, Melissa, Anja, Dena, Adrienne, Barb, Joanne, Daphne, Nancy, and the rest of the Maritime Modern Quilt Guild, thank you for your constant support and encouragement from Day One of my quilting journey. Gillian and Jeanette—being in step with me as quilters and as friends and ahead of me in life experience—your opinions and care mean a lot.

To the quilters who made pieced fabric into quilts for this book—Sheri, Gillian, Nancy, and Carolyn—your expertise fills a gap in mine.

To our Kickstarter backers, for believing that this book was worth making and for cheering me on. To the Toronto Modern Quilt Guild, the York Heritage Quilters Guild, and The Sewing Cafe for your collective support. And to Mad About Patchwork and Aurifil for supporting the Kickstarter generously and with enthusiasm.

And finally, to my family—Colin, Leo, and Simon—and to my parents, for giving me a home to always come back to.

Opposite: *Fogo II* with its vintage sheet backing.

Resources

TEMPLATE DOWNLOADS
3rdstoryworkshop.com/quilting-book

ARTISTS AND QUILTERS

Quilt Art, Curation, and the Women of Color Quilters Network
Carolyn Mazloomi / carolynlmazloomi.com
Instagram: @carolynlmazloomi

Improvisational Quilts
Sherri Lynn Wood / sherrilynnwood.com
Instagram: @sherrilynnwood

Sheila Frampton Cooper / zoombaby.com
Instagram: @sheilaframptoncooper

Émilie Trahan / Instagram: @mili.tra

Denyse Schmidt / dsquilts.com
Instagram: @dsquilts

Speed Date with Improv
Krista Hennebury
poppyprintcreates.blogspot.com
Instagram: @poppyprint

Bias Tape Appliqué
Emily Watts / emilywattsquilts.com
Instagram: @emilywattsquilts

Fibre Art Explorations
Gillian Noonan / Instagram: @sewgolly

Collective Voice
Kim Soper / lelandavestudios.com
Instagram: @lelandavestudios

Inset Strips
Stephanie Ruyle
spontaneousthreads.blogspot.com
Instagram: @spontaneousthreads

Inset Curves
Jenny Haynes / pappersaxsten.com
Instagram: @pappersaxsten

Abstract Underpainting
Katie Straus / katiestraus.com
Instagram: @katiestraus_art

Helen Wells / helenwellsartist.com
Instagram: @helenwellsart

Slabs
Cheryl Arkison / cherylarkison.com
Instagram: @cherylarkison

Amanda Jean Nyberg
crazymomquilts.blogspot.com
Instagram: @crazymomquilts

Quilt Shows, Exhibitions, and Mounting Work
Kelly Spell / kellyspell.squarespace.com
@kellyspell

TUTORIALS

Inset Strips
"How do you feel about a little stripping?"
Spontaneous Threads, Stephanie Ruyle, March 11, 2015, spontaneousthreads.blogspot.com/2015/03/how-do-you-feel-about-little-stripping.html

Scant 1/4" Seam Allowance
"What is a scant 1/4" seam allowance?" Andrea Tsang Jackson, April 19, 2019, 3rdstoryworkshop.com/tutorial-what-is-a-scant-1-4

Mounting a Quilt on Canvas
"Tutorial: How to Mount a Quilt on Canvas," Kelly Spell, November 7 2023, kellyspell.squarespace.com/blog/how-to-mount-a-quilt-on-canvas-tutorial

Foundation Paper Piecing (FPP) Tutorials

- Beginner video tutorial from Ellis Lane Handmade: youtube.com/watch?v=H_w35u9gICk

- Andrea's video tutorial: youtu.be/5IeJmET7PlM

- A collection of Paper Piecing Tips from Quiet Play: quietplay.blogspot.com/p/tutorials.html

Freezer Paper Piecing Tutorial

"Freezer Paper Piecing Tutorial," Rebecca Bryan, February 17, 2023, bryanhousequilts.com/2023/02/freezer-paper-piecing-tutorial-3/.

SUPPLIES

For specific supplies related to the *Trellis* quilt, visit Andrea's online shop: 3rdstoryworkshop.com/quilting-book#supplies

For other supplies, visit your favourite local or online quilt or craft store.

TOOLS

11 Printable Grid Papers

3rdstoryworkshop.com/quilting-book#grid-papers

PreQuilt

Links to PreQuilt's digital layouts and tools for *Trellis*, *House*, and *Era: Boler*, as well as digital versions of the traditional blocks listed in *Fogo II*: 3rdstoryworkshop.com/quilting-book

ORGANIZATIONS

National AIDS Memorial, aidsmemorial.org

Quilts of Valour, quiltsofvalour.ca

Quilts for Survivors, quiltsforsurvivors.ca

Social Justice Sewing Academy, sjsacademy.org

BOOKS

De St-Exupéry, Antoine. *The Little Prince*. Reynal & Hitchcock, 1943.

Gilbert, Elizabeth. *Big Magic: Creative Living Beyond Fear*. Bloomsbury Publishing, 2016.

Glass, Alison. *Alison Glass Appliqué: The Essential Guide to Modern Appliqué*. Lucky Spool Media, 2014.

Lewis, Sarah. *The Rise: Creativity, The Gift of Failure, and The Search for Mastery*. Simon & Schuster, 2015.

Nyberg, Amanda Jean, and Cheryl Arkison. *Sunday Morning Quilts: 16 Modern Scrap Projects – Sort, Store, and Use Every Last Bit of Your Treasured Fabrics*. C&T Publishing, 2012.

Tsang Jackson, Andrea. *Patchwork Lab: Gemology*. Lucky Spool Media, 2019.

WEBSITES / ARTICLES

"Cooperatives," World Quilts: The American Story, International Quilt Museum, accessed August 14, 2024, worldquilts.quiltstudy.org/americanstory/creativity/cooperatives.

"History of the Boler," Boler-Camping, accessed August 22, 2024, boler-camping.com/portfolio/history-of-the-boler.

Bosshardt, William, and Jane S. Lopus. "Business in the Middle Ages: What Was the Role of Guilds?" *Social Education* 77(2), 64–67. National Council for Social Studies, 2013. socialstudies.org/system/files/publications/articles/se_77021364.pdf.

Schwab, Katharine. "See the top-secret suburbs that built America's nuclear weapons." *Fast Company*, June 13, 2018. fastcompany.com/90175737/see-the-top-secret-suburbs-that-built-americas-nuclear-weapons

Soper, Kim. "In Our Own Words, A Finished Quilt." November 27, 2018. lelandavestudios.com/2018/11/27/in-our-own-words-a-finished-quilt/.

Index

Note: Images in the Quests section are included in the page range associated with a particular quilt or topic, unless an image is of a quilt not associated with a Quest, or credits a particular quilter or quilting business other than the author. Images are indicated by page numbers in **bold**. Headings in italics refer to names of quilts unless otherwise indicated. Footnotes are indicated by the page number followed by "n."